Special thank you to these AMAZING librarians who are doing so much to encourage the love of reading and books: Diane Dellicott, Lesley Hurworth and Nicola McDonald.

Published in the UK by Scholastic, 2023
1 London Bridge, London, SE1 9BG
Scholastic Ireland, 89E Lagan Road, Dublin Industrial Estate,
Glasnevin, Dublin, D11 HP5F

ISBN 978-93-5471-730-7

A CIP catalogue record for this book is available from the British Library.

Printed and bound in India by Saurabh Printers Pvt. Ltd.

This reprint edition, August 2025

www.scholastic.co.uk

By Liz Pichon

Hidden in the book are

these FIVE funny star bugs

for you to FIND.

Answers on p.227. Don't cheat!

A MASSIVE thank-you to all these super-skilled folk for helping to make this Tom Gates book and for getting the books out into the world. You are all AMAZING!

My publisher Scholastic and all the lovely people there. Lauren, Catherine, Sarah, Jason, Andrew, Penelope, Claire, Toni, and the Scholastic Warwick Team!

My sister Lyn. Mark (as ever!).

Thanks to all the librarians, booksellers teachers, parents and anyone who has read or recommended a Tom Gates book.

Much love,
Liz XXXX

Derek and I have invented this SILLY game. We play it any time we can - just for a "LAUGH". The whole point of the game is to STARE at NOTHING and see how many kids we can get to copy us.
Derek staring

Derek starts with...
Did you see THAT, TOM?
WHAT?
I say EXCITEDLY.
LOOK UP THERE!
Derek points to the skies.
WOW!
I say and pull a face like I've just seen the most BRILLIANT thing EVER.
Marcus hears us and wants to know what's going on.
What are you two STARING at?
We've just seen something AMAZING!
1
Derek replies in a very convincing way.

Go on - TELL ME!
Marcus is KEEN to know.
Well, we think we saw...
It could have been...
Derek is really stringing this out!
Then I join in.
I'm SURE it's what we think it is.
It DID look JUST like one.
WHAT DID YOU SEE?
cross
Marcus is getting annoyed.
Well, we think we saw a...
(Derek pauses for dramatic effect...)
... a UFO,
I finally say.
REALLY?
How do you know?
Marcus asks, all WIDE-EYED
and interested.

Marcus is looking UP and keeps checking the sky. Ross White comes along with Trevor Peters and Norman. Two younger kids are behind them.

Trevor asks.

We SAW something hovering in the sky,

Derek explains.

Norman takes off his glasses and wipes the lenses on his arm, then puts them back on.

NOPE, still can't see anything.

"It was probably an aeroplane,"

one little kid suggests sensibly.

BUT it was shaped like this – like an ACTUAL spaceship.

Derek uses his fingers to draw the shape of the spaceship in front of him.

Then he **GASPS** and says,

"YES, I SAW IT TOO!"

I join in.

(Derek is SO good at this game.)

"What ARE YOU TWO looking AT? I can only see clouds."

Marcus thinks he's missed the UFO and he's annoyed about it.

The bell goes for the start of school. Ding Ding Ding

AMY, Florence and Indrani want to get past,

but we're blocking the way. "Move, please," AMY says, but everyone's looking up and no one budges.

"Hey, AMY, we just saw a real UFO. That's an UNIDENTIFIED FLYING OBJECT!

We're waiting to see if it comes back," Marcus explains.

AMY doesn't look up, but Florence does...

... and so does Indrani.

"It could have been a **UFCP**," Indrani says.

"What's a **UFCP**?" I ask.

"**U**nidentified **F**lying **C**risp **P**acket. When it's *windy* and some rubbish flies out of the bin and up into the air. Come on, let's go. There's nothing there. See you in class."

Indrani LAUGHS.

"THIS is RIDICULOUS!" Marcus huffs and follows them into school.

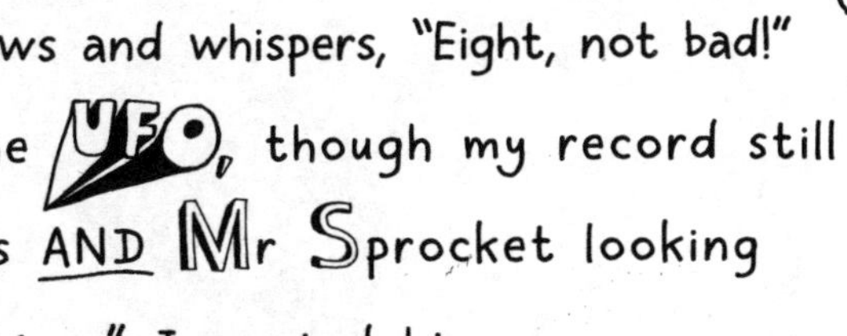

Derek raises his eyebrows and whispers, "Eight, not bad!"

"Good thinking on the UFO, though my record still stands at twelve kids AND Mr Sprocket looking down a drain at nothing," I remind him.

Oh yeah... That was a good one.
Hmmm, keep looking...

"I might have to pretend there's a UFO again," Derek tells me. "It was GENIUS!

See you at break time."

As he heads off to Mr Sprocket's class, I call out,

"HEY, Derek - whatever you do, don't turn around."

(He turns around.)

"Ha! Got you..." I LAUGH.

"Every time... Nice one, Tom."

Mr Fullerman is at the back of the class, handing out today's worksheet. I sit down next to AMY and Marcus.

Straight away, Marcus says,

"You didn't REALLY see a UFO, did you?"

(He's still cross with me.)

"Yes, we did, or we *thought* we did."

"You just like playing silly games," Marcus grumbles.

For a change, AMY agrees with Marcus.

"He's got a point, Tom."

"What do you mean?" I try and sound SURPRISED.

"You and Derek play a game where you look at NOTHING and see how many kids copy you,"

AMY calls me out.

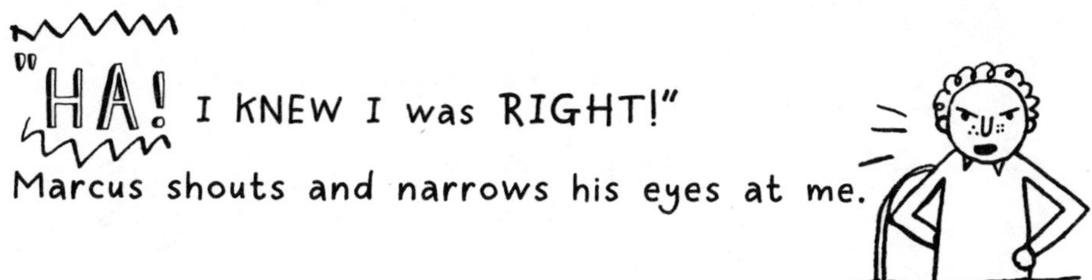

"HA! I KNEW I was RIGHT!"

Marcus shouts and narrows his eyes at me.

"Sometimes we really DO see things!"

I say, but I'm not sure anyone believes me.

Then AMY nudges me.

"HEY – what's Caretaker Stan doing in the school grounds? Is he ... dancing?" she asks us.

Marcus and I turn to look out of the window ...

... at nothing.

"You're right - this game is FUN!"
AMY LAUGHS to herself.

"I didn't look. I was watching Tom,"
Marcus mutters.

(He did look.) ☹

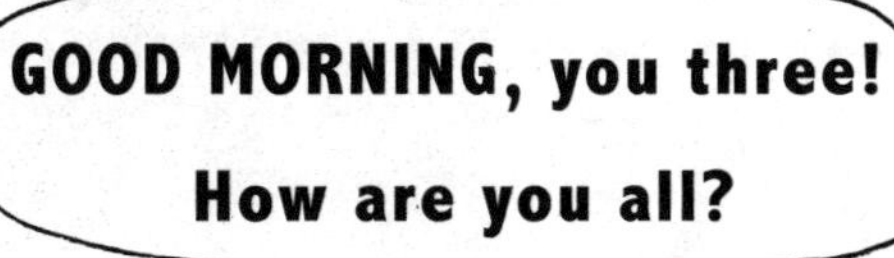

Mr Fullerman says cheerily and hands us a worksheet each.

For some reason, Marcus decides to tell him all about the game we've been playing.

"Sir, sir, Tom and AMY have been making up stories, sir. They keep getting me to look at things that aren't really there."

"EXCELLENT! Just what I want to hear. Today is all about making up stories."

Marcus is pulling faces like he doesn't understand.

"Sir?"

"You're **ALL** going to be writing FUNNY stories!" Mr Fullerman explains.

"What kind of funny stories, sir?"

"Ones that make you LAUGH, Marcus!"

Then AMY reads the worksheet out.

"Listen up, both of you..."

OAKFIELD SCHOOL'S
FIVE-STAR
* * * * *
FUNNY STORIES
We want you to write a
FUNNY STORY
for Oakfield School's first
EVER story book.
Write about anything that
makes YOU laugh, and if
your teacher gives you
* * * * * FIVE STARS,
your story will be
included in the book.

Here are some TIPS to get you started:

- Write about something that's made you laugh or that you find fun.
- Don't make your story too long.
- Read it out loud when you finish writing it.
- You could also write a funny poem too.
- Now – what are you waiting for? Get writing and

MAKE US LAUGH!

*****

Marcus looks like he's plotting what to write about already.

"My story will be SO FUNNY! Do you want to know what it's about?" he asks.

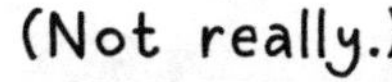

I'll start like this: once upon a time, there were some RIDICULOUS, ANNOYING kids who pretended to see UFOs. But really, they were just BUFFOONS who liked making things up.

"Isn't a BUFFOON an animal?" I ask.

Marcus stops talking for a second.

?

"Errrr, no."

"You've got loads of <u>other</u> FUNNY stories to tell, Marcus. Don't write about US," I say.

"It's the ONLY FUNNY story I can think of right now," he says.

"Really? I can think of LOADS."

Then I remind him of a few.

"What about the time we went on the bug-collecting school trip and you fell in the mud? That was FUNNY!"

"Oh, yes, that WAS FUNNY!" AMY agrees. "And remember when you both got stuck on the boating lake and the birds came and ate your sandwiches, Marcus?"

"It wasn't that funny," Marcus grumbles.

(It really was.)

"How about when we thought you had a HUGE dog, but Tiny turned out to be ... tiny."

AMY and I are giggling a bit too loudly and **Mr Fullerman GLARES** in our direction.

"I HOPE you're laughing at the story you're about to write?"

beady eyes

"Sort of, sir..." I say quickly.

Marcus puts his hand up again to tell **Mr Fullerman** something else.

Sir!
Sir!
Sir!

"Yes, Marcus?"

"Errrr ... I've forgotten," Marcus says,

so **Mr Fullerman** moves on and CLAPS his hands to get everyone's attention.

CLAP CLAP

Marcus is still trying to remember what he wanted to say.

"Norman, glasses ON your face, please. Amber, take the pencil OUT of your mouth. Brad, don't do that. Brad! Right, Class 5F, at today's assembly, we're all in for a TREAT!"

When I hear the word TREAT, I think he's talking about something to eat and I get excited.

I hear myself saying **OUT LOUD**, "I LOVE TREATS!" (I'm not the only one.) Brad shouts from the back of the class,

Everyone CHEERS at the idea of getting biscuits in assembly.

Hooray!

"No, not biscuits, Brad, something even BETTER."

(What's better than biscuits?)

"Mrs Nap has a brand-new song to teach us that includes a bit of..."

Brad tries again.

"Not cake, Brad. WHISTLING," Mr Fullerman says. **"AND the recycled instrument orchestra will be joining in,"** he adds like that's a good thing.

Everyone in the class starts to *whistle* to show Mr Fullerman they can do it.

(Apart from me. I don't know why but I can't *whistle*.)

whistle whistle whistle whistle whistle whistle

(me not *whistling*)

"Excellent whistling. Now let's see if you can all stand up and push your chairs in..."

SCRAPE SCRAPE SCRAPE SCRAPE SCRAPE SCRAPE SCRAPE

"QUIETLY..."

Mr Fullerman says, but it's hard to hear over the noise of the chairs and *whistling*.

There's (still) a LOT of tuneless *whistling* going on as we walk to assembly. Marcus is doing it right next to my EAR.

"I love *whistling*. It's so easy.

See. *Whistle*."

He keeps doing it...

I try and ignore him when I notice there's a BIG BLOB of chewing gum on the floor.

Using my EXPERT swerving skills, I avoid the gum and I warn Marcus because I am a good person.

"Hey, Marcus. Look out for the–"

"Nice try, Tom. I'm not falling for that TRICK again," he says ...

... and steps right in the gum.

"WHO PUT THAT THERE?"

Marcus tries to BLAME me for the gum. Now every time he takes a step it gets STUCK. At least he's stopped *whistling* now.

SIR, I've got chewing gum on the bottom of my shoe.

Mr Fullerman hands him a tissue.

For goodness' sake, Marcus, hurry up. Mrs Nap is waiting for us to sit down.

Marcus has to hop the rest of the way, then sits down dramatically like his foot's been injured. He grumbles as he tries to get the gum off.

This is ridiculous.

"I did try and tell you. You didn't listen to me," I enjoy reminding him.

Mrs Nap is looking especially HAPPY today, chatting to the recycled instrument orchestra kids who are ready to play their "guitars". They look like they're made from cardboard boxes, elastic bands and sticky tape. (LOTS of sticky tape.)

I think, but I don't say it out loud.

"Good morning. Is everyone OK?" Mrs Nap asks us.

"Yes, Mrs Nap," we all say.

Marcus is still grumbling about his sticky gum foot.

"Today I'll be teaching you my BRAND-NEW SONG!" she says excitedly.

"Can you all whistle?" she asks, which makes the whole school start *whistling* very tunelessly.

Everyone joins in ... apart from me. I keep trying but nothing that sounds like a *whistle* is coming out.

Mrs Nap *whistles* the simple tune for us to copy.

whistle *whistle* *whistle* *whistle* *whistle* *whistle*

She repeats it a few times, but I've given up.

rrrasssp

"Anyone who can't whistle, clap your hands instead!" she says, looking straight at me.

"After FOUR, everyone.

One, two..."

CLAP CLAP CLAP

The recycled orchestra starts too **EARLY** and there are already a few elastic bands pinging and twanging...

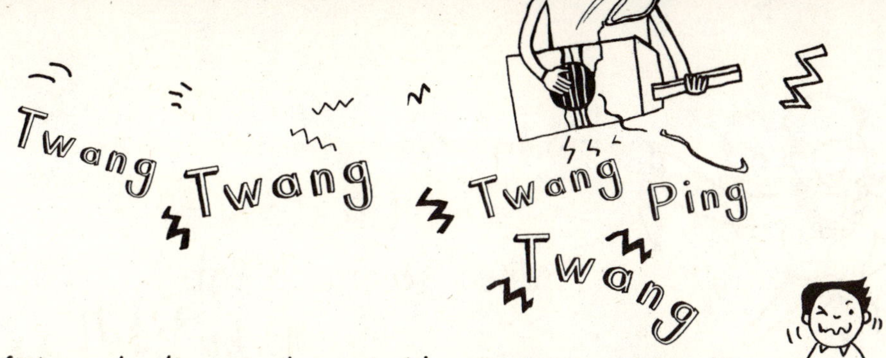

(They don't sound much like guitars, either.)

I'm doing my best not to LAUGH as I don't want to get into trouble with Mr Fullerman or get the

STARE OF DOOM.

Looking around at the other teachers in the hall, I can see I'm not the only one trying not to LAUGH.

Meanwhile ... Mrs Nap is trying her very best to teach us the NEW SONG.

(This is going to be a very long assembly...)

"Don't feel gloomy
Don't feel sad,
There's so much fun
to be **had!**
Forget all the things
That make you bristle,
Sing along with me,
It's time to WHISTLE."

Mrs Nap sings the song over and over and over again. She wants the song to get stuck in our heads so we remember it. (It's working.)

Everyone around me is having no problem at all *whistling* away.

Marcus is *whistling* AND looking smug at the same time.

I do a pretend *whistle* without making a sound to blend in, which sort of works.

Mrs Nap does her best to try and keep us all on track, but it's a bit ...  difficult.

She's doing a lot of POINTING  and encouraging FACIAL EXPRESSIONS at the recycled orchestra as they carry on PINGING.

Finally, Mrs Nap brings us to a STOP with her hands and one more elastic band pings from one of the "guitars".

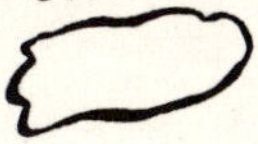

"That was TERRIBLE," AMY says and pulls a face at me.

"It was sort of FUNNY, though, wasn't it?" I point out.

Then Marcus suddenly *LEANS* in and adds,

"You can't whistle, can you, Tom?"

"Eeeerrrr, yes I can."

"Go on then?"

Before Marcus forces me to *whistle,*

another **PINGING** elastic band flies through the air and

Mrs Worthington **CATCHES** it with one hand!

We all **CHEER!**

It's the best thing about assembly.

(So far.)

Mrs Worthington takes a BOW, then holds up the same book Mr Fullerman showed us.

"Right, Oakfield School, do you all know what this is?" she asks.

someone (Brad Galloway) shouts from the back of the hall.

"Yes, but what kind of book is it?"

A small BOOK!

Mrs Worthington ignores Brad and begins to explain about the **school story book** and how we should all have a go at writing something FUNNY.

A little kid right at the front puts up their hand.

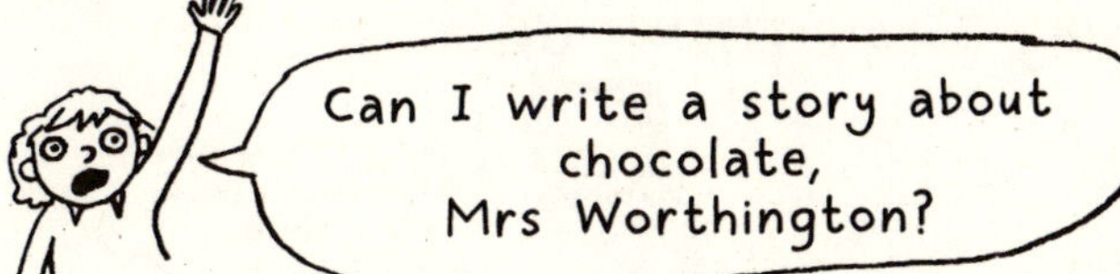

"Yes, of course, Dawn. Who wouldn't want to read a story about chocolate?"

"ME! I don't like chocolate," some other kid shouts from the back.

(I GASP. Who knew that was even possible?)

Then Norman puts up his hand.

"Can I write about Dragons and cheese, Mrs Worthington?"

"That sounds exciting, Norman, but not all the stories have to include food," she replies.

Now Mrs Worthington's said "FOOD", that's the only thing I can THINK of.

I really want MY story to get into the book. What can I write about that Mr Fullerman will give me FIVE STARS for?

I'm trying to remember OTHER FUNNY STORIES I have. Some I probably shouldn't write about. Like the time I drew a picture of Mr Fullerbum on the back of my homework (accidentally).

OR when I called Mrs Worthington "Mum" by mistake, and she saw the EXTREME close-up picture I drew of her.

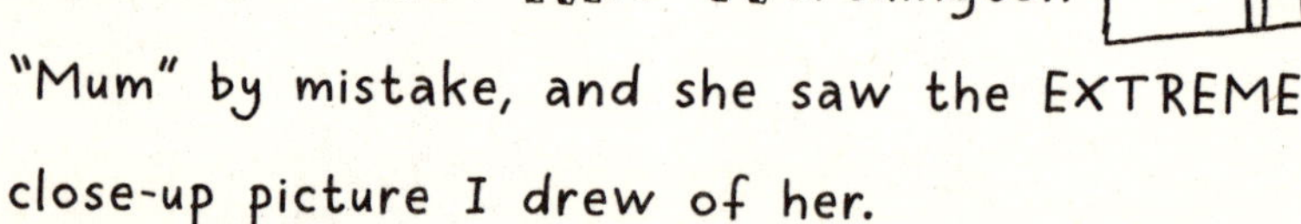

I got a detention for that.

Oh ... and the time I drew Mr Keen's eyebrows as caterpillars.

I'm not sure I'd get FIVE STARS for any of those ideas.

thinking face

At break time, I ask around to see what everyone else is going to write about.

"I might do a story about Rooster – he's ALWAYS doing something FUNNY," Derek tells me.

(True.)

Leroy tells us a story about his dad, who used to pretend that money could come out of his EARS like MAGIC.

"I believed him for AGES!" Leroy says.

"Does it have to be a REAL story?" Florence asks.

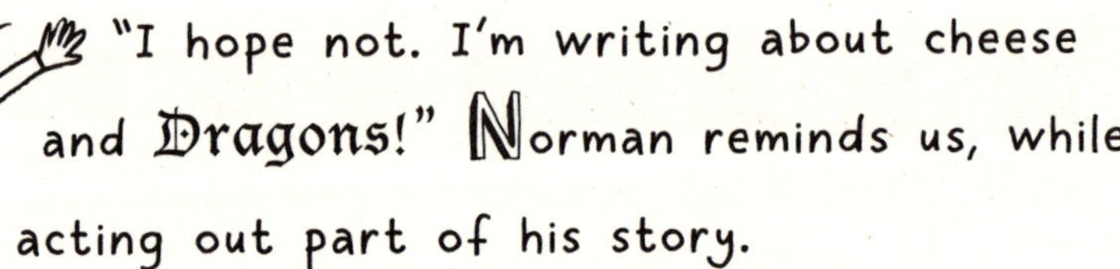

"I hope not. I'm writing about cheese and Dragons!" Norman reminds us, while acting out part of his story.

Everyone seems to have good ☺ ideas for their stories apart from ME.

"You'll think of something, Tom," Derek assures me. I hope so.

The rest of the day I keep trying
to THINK of a story.
In P.E. class.
Ideas...
Ideas...
What to write?
Tom, catch!
At lunchtime.
What's in your sandwich?
Giant sandwich?
During lessons.
Holiday.
No school for two weeks just for FUN!
SIR!

Even when school's finished and I'm walking home, I'm still trying to think of story ideas. But I don't know **what** I can write about.

My mind's gone **BLANK**. I wish I could get some **INSPIRATION** from somewhere?

But nothing's happening.

When I get home, I go straight to the kitchen to check the fridge. Delia's already there so I STOP. She's obviously not going to move, so I decide to ask her a question.

"Delia, Deeelia."

"What do you want, Tom?"

"If you had to write a FUNNY STORY, what would you write about?"

"Let me think... I know! Your school photos always make me LAUGH," she says.

"Very FUNNY." I sigh.

"Yes, they are." Delia smiles.

Then she says...

"Why don't you go and look in your room for inspiration, Tom? You might find something FUNNY up there."

I know Delia is trying to get rid of me, but it's not such a bad idea.

"Or take a look in the mirror. That might give you an idea for a FUNNY STORY," she says.

"Ha ha, you're HILARIOUS."

"I know. Thanks, Tom."

I go to my room and have a look around at all my collections. Like my stone collection.

That's when I get an IDEA.

I could write a FUNNY story about HOW I got this stone. It's my special stone and I bring it everywhere with me (if I remember to).

But then again ...

... there's always

Great-Aunt Aggie's fake bird hat.

I keep it on top of my wardrobe so the fake birds look down at me.

Maybe I should write about how I got the hat?

(Suddenly, I'm getting LOTS of good ideas.)

The hat used to belong to Granddad Bob's ***Great-Aunt Aggie.*** I've seen pictures of

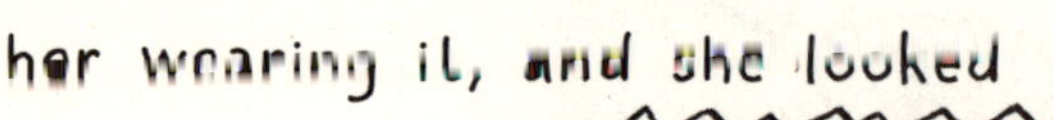

her wearing it, and she looked

FIERCE.

Delia thinks the hat is creepy.

"It's not creepy. Granddad says it's LUCKY," I told her.

"Not for those birds it wasn't," Delia said.

"They're FAKE birds, not real birds," I reminded her.

If Granddad ever asks Mum about the hat, she gets it down so Granddad can see we're looking after it.

This hat COULD be a good story for the book. But would it be FUNNY enough to get me

? (Maybe.)

FIVE STARS, TOM!
Ha!
The Fake Bird Hat
By
TOM GATES
Ha! Ha!
Ha!
Ha! Ha!
Ha!
Ha!

My Five-Star Funny Story
Great-Aunt Aggie's Fake Bird Hat
by Tom Gates
HA! HA!
HA! HA!

One day a ***posh***-looking envelope dropped through our letter box. It had a red wax seal on the back and the address was written in very ***fancy*** handwriting. I gave it to Mum, who was excited to open it.

"What's that?" I asked.

"Something special, I hope," Mum said.

I've never seen her JUMP up and down like that about a letter.

"Have we won the **LOTTERY**?" I asked.

"No, Tom – I think we've been invited to a super ***fancy*** party," she told me.

"BRILLIANT! I LOVE parties!" I said.

"Sorry, Tom, no kids allowed."

"Huh?" This was a **SHOCK.**

"Why can't I come?"

"It's just for grown-ups. You wouldn't enjoy it anyway," Mum tried to explain.

I might.

Mum took the invitation to show Dad, who was outside working in the shed, leaving the envelope behind. I picked it up for a closer look and noticed there was a small card inside.

It said

on one side. There was NOTHING about kids not being allowed.

"Are you SURE I can't come?" I checked when Mum and Dad came back in.

"Totally sure. You might have to stay with Granny and Granddad as Delia's going out that night. That's OK, isn't it?" Mum asked, checking the calendar on the fridge.

I always have a nice time with THE FOSSILS (that's what I call my grandparents, in case you don't know). Dad seemed EXCITED about the party as well.

"You'll have to get something smarter to wear," Mum told him.

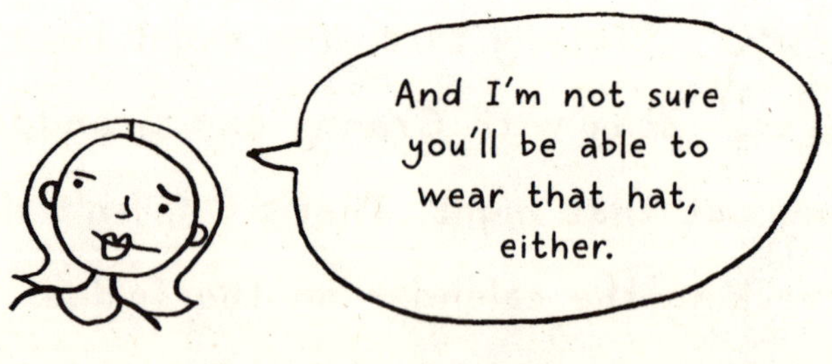

"What's wrong with my old suit, and that T-shirt with the BOW TIE drawn on, these trainers and my hat, Rita?" Dad asked seriously before he started to LAUGH.

"Don't worry - I'm still wearing the hat, though," he added.

Mum wasn't smiling.

I knew the party must be a BIG deal when Dad hired a SUIT and then told Uncle Kevin and Aunty Alice all about the invite when they popped round.

TOP SUITS

"Wait, you're going to *THAT* party?" Uncle Kevin said, in a very surprised way.

"Yes, we are. Didn't you get an invitation?" Dad smiled.

"We did, but we can't go. We're busy."

"You might be busy, but I'm not," Aunty Alice muttered.

(I think Aunty Alice really wanted to go to the party.)

furious

When Delia heard about the *fancy* PARTY, the first thing she said was,

"I'm not babysitting. I've got PLANS."

"I'm staying at Granny and Granddad's ... AND I'm not a baby," I said quickly so she couldn't **grumble** at me. It's not **FUN** for anyone when Delia babysits – especially ME.

On the night of the party, Mum and Dad took AGES to get ready. I'd packed a bag EARLY with all the IMPORTANT stuff like my stone collection and comics. Mum and Dad were going to

TREAT us to a takeaway so Granny Mavis didn't have to cook anything ODD with bits in.

bits

It was getting later and later and I was still waiting when Mum called out:

FRANK! Don't forget to bring the invitation. We need it to get into the party!

Dad didn't answer at first. He was too busy dancing in front of the mirror.

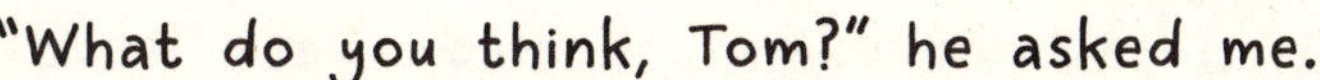

"What do you think, Tom?" he asked me.

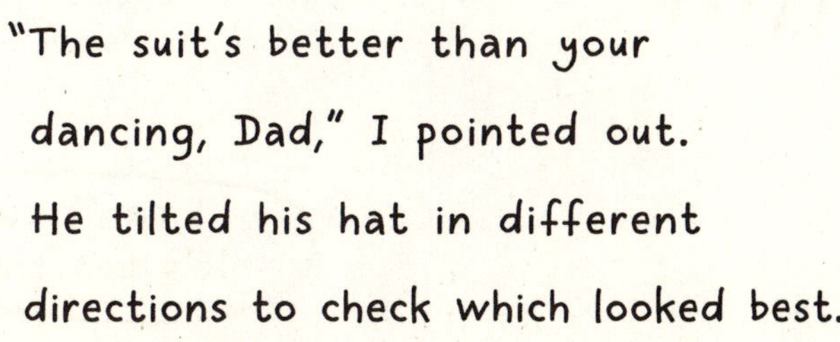

"The suit's better than your dancing, Dad," I pointed out. He tilted his hat in different directions to check which looked best.

Then, as he tried to get Mum to dance with him,

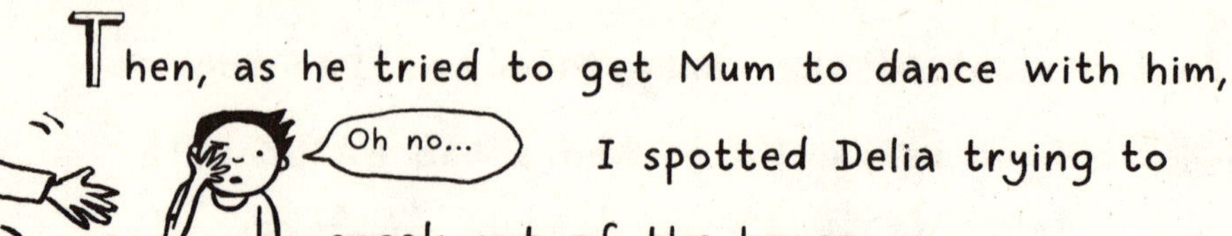

I spotted Delia trying to sneak out of the house.

Obviously, I shouted,

"Message us when you get home and don't be late," Mum told her.

Dad showed her a few of his dance moves, which made Delia leave even faster.

I followed her all the way to the front door and asked some questions (because Delia loves that).

"Where EXACTLY are you going?"

"Do you like wafers more than cakes?"

"What time are you coming home?"

"Don't you like dancing?"

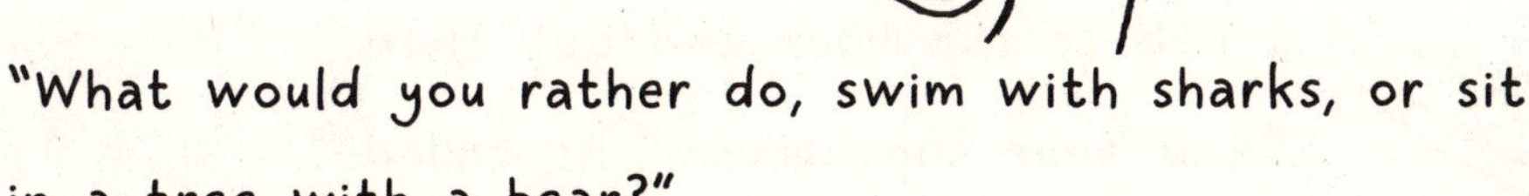

"What would you rather do, swim with sharks, or sit in a tree with a bear?"

"Why didn't you want to say goodbye?"

BYE!

BYE, TOM.

BYE!

BYE, DELIA!

I waved goodbye to her. It was like she couldn't get away fast enough.

Dad stopped dancing and carried my overnight bag to the car.

"What have you got in here? It weighs a

."

"Just all the IMPORTANT things I need," I explained.

"Like your pyjamas?" Dad checked.

I had to run back and get them.

"And your toothbrush!" he called.

(I had to go back for that too.)

Normally, if I'm staying the night somewhere, Mum and Dad fuss a LOT more. But they were both in such a **GOOD MOOD** they even let me choose the music in the car. We had a nice singsong all the way to THE FOSSILS' house.

We even sat in the car until the song finished.

Granny Mavis was wondering why we took so long to get out of the car.

"Don't you all look FANTASTIC!" she told us as we walked inside.

I said, "Thanks," even though I wasn't going to the party.

"They all scrub up well! Just like me!" Granddad added.

Mum and Dad thanked THE FOSSILS for having me and then said they needed to leave.

"I've been told latecomers get the worst seats," Dad said.

Granny was being very organized and called them a taxi. Then Mum checked again...

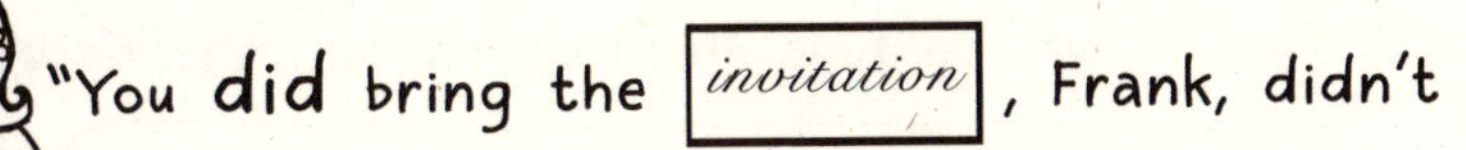

"You **did** bring the *invitation*, Frank, didn't you?"

Dad enjoyed patting his pockets, looking for a bit longer than he should have done.

(It was under his hat.)

"As if I'd forget the invitation, Rita!" Dad smiled.

"Did you know your GALA DINNER was in the local paper? Apparently, there'll be lots of VERY IMPORTANT people there," Granny said, taking a look at the invitation.

"Important people LIKE US," Dad added, and Mum rolled her eyes.

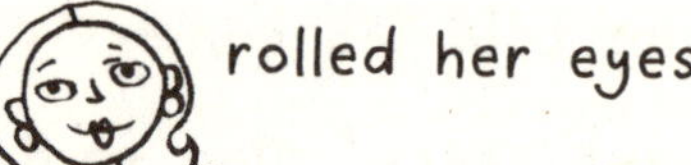

They both gave me a hug as the taxi arrived. "Be good, Tom!" Mum said as she headed out the door.

NO! YOU CAN'T GO!

I shouted dramatically, which made them STOP.

"WHAT'S WRONG?" Dad said.

"It's only one night," Mum added.

"Granny's got your invitation!" I passed it over and a small card fell on the floor.

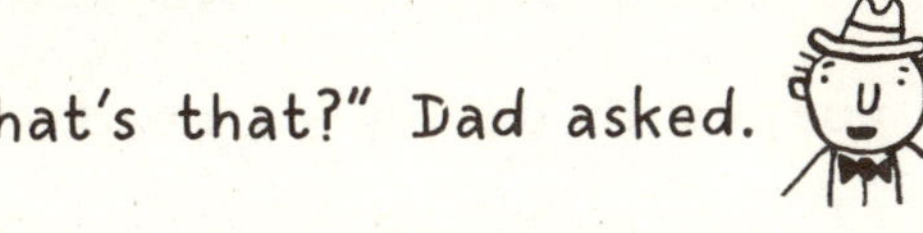

"What's that?" Dad asked.

"It's just the dress code card," I said and picked it up.

Dress code: this year's theme is hats. Please dress smartly and WEAR A HAT. There will be a photographer on the night.

Mum froze.

"HATS? HATS? WHAT HATS?"

she said.

Mum kept saying the word "HATS" like she didn't know what a hat was.

"Where am I going to get a hat NOW?" she asked in a panic.

Dad pointed to his own hat and suggested, "Hey, we can share mine. No one will notice." he popped it on Mum's head.

I'll ask the taxi to wait...

Then I had an IDEA. I pointed to the pegs. "Mum, you could wear one of THOSE hats!"

"Good thinking, Tom!" Dad went to grab a selection.

"You're welcome to wear any of our hats, Rita," Granddad told her.

This was a HAT **EMERGENCY** after all.

"Try this." Dad gave Mum the first hat.

"If you turn it round, it won't say BOB on the front," I pointed out.

"I can't wear a bobble hat to a gala dinner. No offence, Bob."

None taken.

Mum was trying not to get stressed and tried on the other hats as quickly as she could.

Dad said the flat cap looked "edgy". Mum didn't agree.

The straw boater was too big and had holes in it.

"I can make a paper hat for you, Mum!" I suggested.

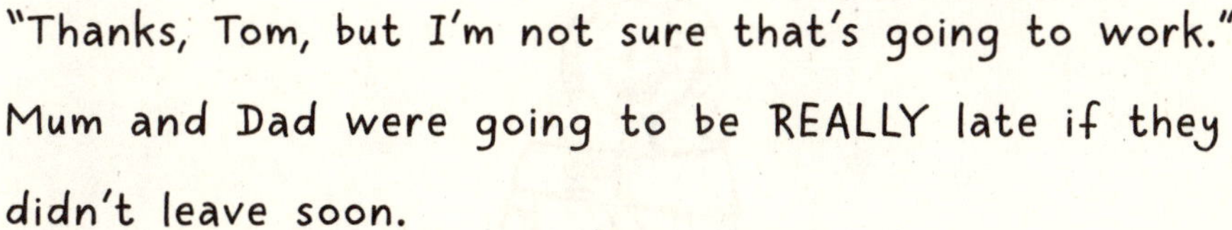

"Thanks, Tom, but I'm not sure that's going to work." Mum and Dad were going to be REALLY late if they didn't leave soon.

"There's not enough time to go home, and all the shops are closed," Dad announced.

"That's really HELPFUL, Frank." Mum wasn't impressed. We were all thinking of what to do when Granddad shouted,

"RITA! I've GOT IT! Why didn't I think of this before? My *Great-Aunt Aggie's* hat's been in the family for years. I'll go and get it – it's PERFECT!"

"Bob, you're a ★STAR★, thank you! We might even make it to the party on time now!" Mum sounded relieved.

Granddad *rushed* off to get it as fast as he could go.

(Which wasn't very fast.)

Eventually, Granddad reappeared holding a SMART HAT BOX.

"That's such a GREAT IDEA, Bob! You've wanted to pass that hat down for ages," Granny reminded him. "And the taxi's still waiting," she added.

Mum took the box quickly.

"Bob, this is AMAZING. I'm going to wear ***Great-Aunt Aggie's*** hat with PRIDE."

Then she opened the box...

Mum was struggling to speak, so I asked, "Are they REAL BIRDS?"

"NO! They're FAKE. ***Aunt Aggie*** hand sewed everything on to the hat. It took her a very long time. Let me help you put it on, Rita. It's a very precious hat," Granddad said and helped her try it on.

It sounded like the hat meant a LOT to Granddad. The birds did look pretty impressive.

Then Mum put the hat on ...

... and disappeared under the brim.

"Oh no ... it's far too big," Mum called from underneath. We could only see her mouth moving. "I need something to pad it out inside, lift the hat up a bit. Frank, can you help?" Mum asked.

"Don't move, Rita. I've got this."

Dad ran into the kitchen and came back holding ...

Huh?

... two rolls of kitchen paper, which didn't seem like the best idea to me (or Mum).

"Don't panic. Take the hat off," Dad said and started to STUFF the inside of the hat with paper.

"You've got a really tiny head, Rita," he commented. "Let's see if this works."

Mum put the hat back on and with a few more pieces of kitchen roll, the hat fit perfectly (sort of).

"It really suits you, Rita. This hat was MEANT for you. It's been in the box far too long. I'm so glad you can wear it to such a lovely event. You must keep the hat. It's YOURS," Granddad told Mum proudly.

"I couldn't possibly, Bob. The hat belongs in your family."

"You *are* my family, Rita," Granddad reminded Mum.

Dad was tapping his watch. "We'd better go..."

"I'll just have a quick look in the mirror."

"Make sure you can't see the kitchen roll - that wouldn't be..."

"Oh MY GIDDY AUNT..."

Mum said slowly, which didn't make sense because I thought the hat was ***Great-Aunt Aggie's?***

"Think of the party, Rita. You're a TWEET for the eyes," Dad said and LAUGHED.

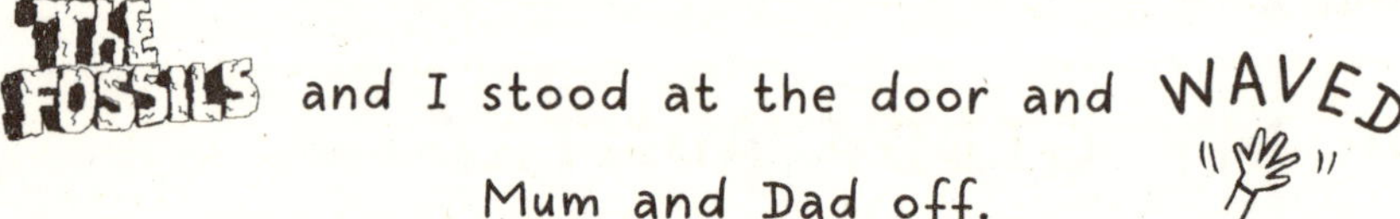

THE FOSSILS and I stood at the door and WAVED Mum and Dad off.

BRING BACK NICE TREATS, PLEASE! LIKE CAKE!

(All good parties have cake, don't they?)

"When I saw your mum wearing that hat, all these memories came flooding back." Granddad sighed.

"Aww, that's nice, Bob." Granny smiled.

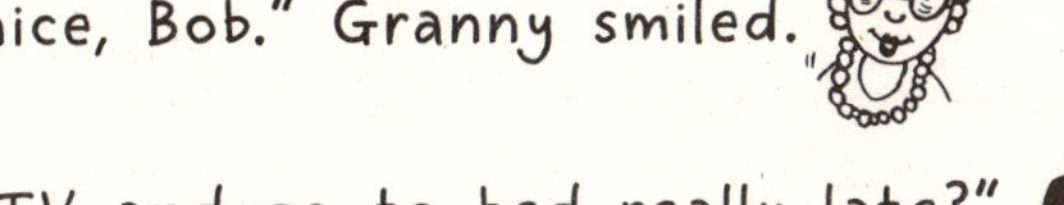

"Can I watch TV and go to bed really late?" I asked hopefully.

Granddad carried on chatting like he wasn't really listening.

So I said it again and this time added in **SNACKS**.

"Can I watch TV, go to bed really late AND eat snacks?"

"Ooh! Snacks. I've got just the thing for us to have, Tom," Granny said.

(Oh...)

Even though Granny might have made odd snacks, this was still going to be an EXCELLENT evening.

I got to choose a film, which was EASY.

SWAMP MONSTER

(Not like at home when we can never

agree what to watch.) ☹

Then Granny ordered pizza while Granddad showed me some old photos of *Great-Aunt Aggie*.

"She was always the life and soul of the party," he said.

(It was hard to believe from the photos.)

We had the **BEST** evening ever watching the film, eating pizza and staying up late (ish).

SWAMP MONSTER 1 was a big hit.

Granny even asked about watching **SWAMP MONSTER 2.**

"Is it as good as this one?" she wondered.

★ ◦ ★ ◦ ★ ◦ ★ ◦ ★ ◦ ★ ◦ ★ ◦ ★ ◦ ★ ◦ ★ ◦

In the end I didn't stay up too late and all the IMPORTANT stuff I'd packed in my case (COMICS, interesting stones, teddy) all helped me get to sleep.

That night I had a dream about a **SWAMP MONSTER**...

... who was wearing a hat made of CAKE.
So the SWAMP MONSTERS ate it.

In the morning, Granny called me down for breakfast nice and late. I was very RELAXED until I saw the pot of STURDY porridge she'd made (with bits in).

"No thanks, Granny."

I found some choco pops instead and had those.

"I hope your mum and dad had a nice time last night," Granny said.

"And I hope *Great-Aunt Aggie's* hat was a big SUCCESS," Granddad added.

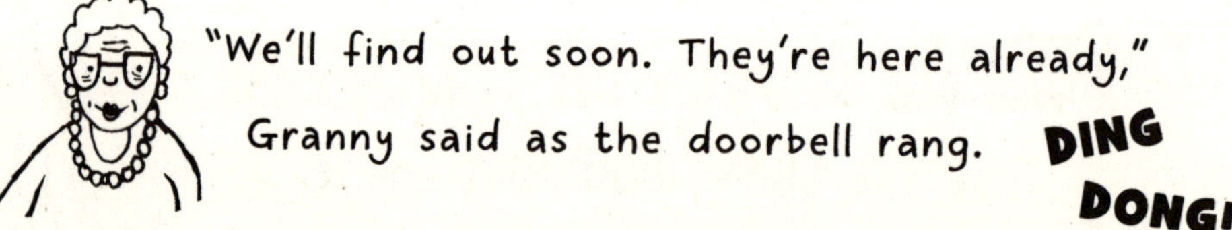

"We'll find out soon. They're here already," Granny said as the doorbell rang. **DING DONG!**

"Awwwwwwwwwwwwww ... do I have to go? We could watch SWAMP MONSTER 2."

"Maybe next time, Tom." Granddad smiled.

I went to get dressed and collect up all my stuff.

When I came down, Mum and Dad were chatting about the party and wanted to know how my evening was.

"TOM! Did you have **FUN**?"

"You didn't keep anyone up snoring, did you?" Dad LAUGHED.

Granddad wanted to know all about *Great-Aunt Aggie's* hat.

"Was the hat a HUGE SUCCESS? Did everyone love it?"

"Everyone loved the hat, Bob."

"You can say that again," Dad said. "It was the talk of the party."

"Yes, it was..." Mum agreed.

"And how about the **CAKE**?" I asked as that was an important question.

No one answered my cake question.

"What were the OTHER hats like?"

Granddad asked.

"Very different to Aunt Aggie's."

Mum LAUGHED.

"It was definitely THE most talked about hat on the night."

"Did anyone talk about CAKE?"

I tried again.

"How about photos? Did anyone take pictures of you wearing the hat, Rita?"

Granddad wanted to know.

"It wasn't that kind of party. Sorry, Bob,"

Mum explained.

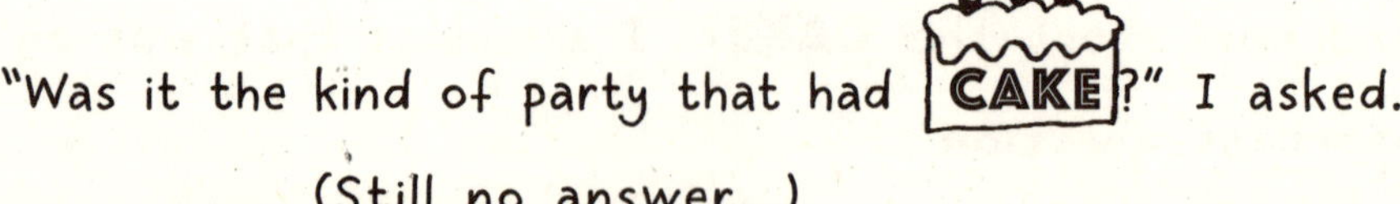

"Was it the kind of party that had CAKE?" I asked.

(Still no answer...)

"What a shame. I'd have loved to have seen you wearing the hat in such a fancy setting, Rita." Granddad sounded a bit sad.

"I'd have LOVED to have seen the CAKE," I added, doing my best.

"Maybe there'll be another party I can wear the hat to?" Mum told Granddad.

"Are you sure about that?" Dad whispered.

"Another party that has CAKE!" I added a bit louder.

Then Granny suddenly said, "HEY! Why don't you ALL come to the **MUSIC NIGHT PARTY** at the LEAFY GREEN OLD FOLKS' HOME? Everyone's going to be dressing up for that. You can wear the hat again, Rita!"

"Oh ... I suppose I could,"

Mum told Granny.

"Really?" Dad asked.

Mum and Dad didn't sound very enthusiastic about another party.

But I WAS!

"Can I come and will there be CAKE?" I checked.

"Yes, Tom, there'll be cake and bow ties, hats and lots of MUSIC.

Of course you can come," Granny said.

"Tea Cup Tony says he'll make a SPECIAL effort to join in the FUN.

It's going to be GREAT," Granddad added.

"Looks like we're going to another party then," Dad said.

Mum didn't seem so excited.

I spotted she was holding what looked like two boxes of ... CAKE?

I shouted.

"It might be. Go and get your bag. Then you can have some."

This made me hurry up.

(I am very snack driven.)

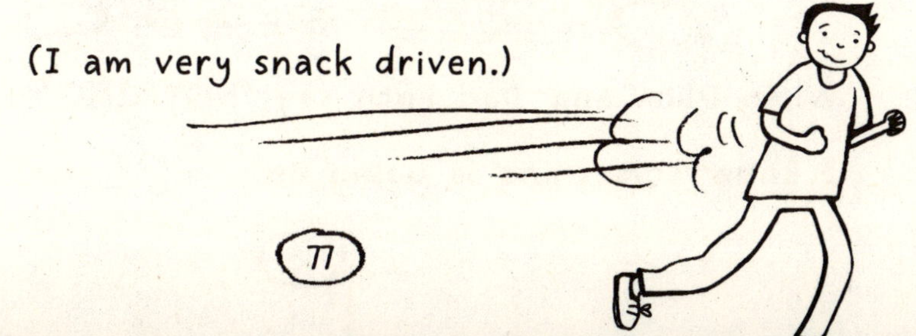

I'd put all my old stones (and some new ones I'd found) in my bag, then said BYE and thank you to THE FOSSILS. "See you at the music party!" Dad complained about my bag being **heavy** (again) as he put it in the car.

On the journey home, I asked the important questions. "Will I need to wear a hat at the LEAFY GREEN party?"

"Maybe. Can you wear the bird hat again, Rita?" Dad asked Mum.

"As long as there are no cats around." Mum LAUGHED.

When Mum and Dad both say "NOTHING" together, I know something is going on.

Especially as they let me eat my cake in the car.

Which was fine by me, but suspicious.

(Normally they don't like the crumbs.)

Dad was still grumbling about my **heavy** bag as he took it upstairs.

I changed the subject and asked,

"Is there any more CAKE?"

"You've had your piece, Tom. Why don't you unpack your bag?" Dad suggested.

Looking for more CAKE seemed like a better idea.

Walking past Mum and Dad's bedroom I SPOTTED *Great-Aunt Aggie's* bird hat on a table.

The hat looked different - and NOT

in a good way...

WHAT HAPPENED TO *Great-Aunt Aggie's* HAT?

Granddad wouldn't be happy about this. I picked up the hat (carefully) and took it downstairs.

"Mum! DAD! THE BIRD HAT'S ALL CRUSHED AND WONKY!" I shouted.

Mum looked surprised.

"TOM! Don't drop it and make it WORSE!"

(Like that was possible.)

"What happened to the hat, Mum?"

"Nothing I can't fix, Tom. Pass it over. I've got the sewing box ready, and Granddad doesn't need to know, OK?" she said.

"Know what? What did you do?" I asked, as I was confused.

"It wasn't ME, Tom. Your dad will explain."

"Dad did it?" I asked.

"NO, I SAVED the hat from looking even WORSE. The CAT did it," Dad said.

"Why was there a cat at the party?"

THIS I had to hear!

Dad tried to explain while Mum tried to fix the hat. Turns out the cat lives at the fancy house where the gala party was being held. (Lucky cat.)

There was a BIG **SCENE**.

The cat MEOWED and tried to eat the birds. Mum shouted, "GET OFF!" and shook her head, which made the cat

CLING ON EVEN MORE!

The birds got badly BASHED UP and bits of kitchen roll fell out. There were feathers everywhere until Mum managed to shake the cat to the floor.

IT WAS CHAOS!

(I wish I'd been there to see it!)

This sounded like THE MOST EXCITING PARTY EVER.

(And the CAKE was delicious too.)

"I need to repair the hat right NOW, Tom. I can't let Granddad see his beloved hat looking like THIS," Mum told me.

"Won't Granddad see the hat at the LEAFY GREEN **Music Night** PARTY?" I wondered.

"I hope not. The hat will be fine by then," Mum said.

"I just HOPE they don't hear about the cat from someone else," Dad added. "And if they do, at least there were no photos as evidence. That's something," he said before Delia came in holding the latest copy of the local paper and smiling.

"Have you seen the front page of the **Oakfield Gazette?** It's a good headline."

Delia held it up, to Mum and Dad's surprise.

Or the cat is," I said.

"Oh no. THE FOSSILS will SEE this and think I've ruined their precious hat!"

"What are you going to do?" I asked.

"The only thing we can," Mum told me.

"Tell Granddad EXACTLY what happened?" I said.

"Not yet..."

Mum and Dad were hoping THE FOSSILS wouldn't SPOT the **headline** in the paper before the hat was fixed.

While Mum fixed ***Great-Aunt Aggie's bird hat,*** Dad went out to get as MANY papers as he could. It took him a while and we ended up with a LOT of papers in our house.

I was looking forward to the

LEAFY GREEN **MUSIC NIGHT PARTY.**

I wore my sunglasses, my DUDE 3 T-shirt, but no hat.

(I'd leave that to Mum and 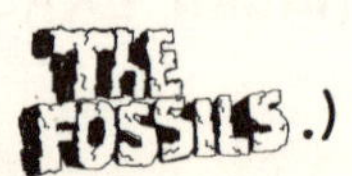.)

The **MUSIC NIGHT** was a **BIG** success. ☺ Everybody in the LEAFY GREEN OLD FOLKS' HOME managed to dress up. Vera wore a **FASCINATOR** which was fascinating with its long feathers.

Tea Cup Tony had a top hat and sang his classic song A nice cup of tea! before heading for a nap. zzzz zzz

Granny and Granddad were DELIGHTED to see Mum wearing ***Great-Aunt Aggie's bird hat.*** Mum had done such a good job of repairing the birds, plumping and sewing things back together, that no one noticed anything different about it. The hat looked almost like it did before...

Almost...

(Just don't look too closely at the birds' eyes.)

The CAKE was PERFECT, though.

I really hope Mr Fullerman will give me five stars for this story.

Now every morning when I wake up I can see the wonky birds and they make me LAUGH. Hopefully Mr Fullerman will LAUGH too.

I do have other things to write about ...

... like my stone collection.

Some stones I keep in boxes and others I put on display or take them with me when I go out.

Derek and I try to find stones that look like other things. I like to paint and draw on them as well. They make good presents for people.

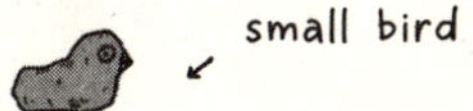

Delia's got quite a few now.

It's a present.

Is it another painted stone? You shouldn't have.

Sometimes she jams them up against her door to stop me from barging into her room.

(It doesn't always work.)

I'm HERE!

"Brilliant..."

CLUNK

This stone is from my "STONE with a HOLE IN" collection. I've drawn on one side of it, and every time I think about how I found it, I LAUGH.

My Five-Star Funny Story
The Special Stone
(And How I Found It)
by
Tom Gates
HA!
HA!
HA!
HA!

At school I did a **SHOW AND TELL** for my class all about my stone collection, which seemed to start a BIG CRAZE on STONES. (These things happen.)

"This stone looks just like Mr Fullerman, especially the EYES."

"Ahem?"

Lots of kids went looking for interesting stones at break time. Caretaker Stan had to ask everyone to

"Stop digging up the flower beds to find stones!"

The STONE CRAZE became so popular that Mrs Mumble even made an announcement over the loudspeaker to say:

"PLEASE DON'T collect STONES from the school grounds, or there will be NONE left! Thank you!"

But now THE WHOLE ENTIRE SCHOOL knew about the STONE CRAZE and it felt like EVERYBODY wanted to join in.

Stones were being traded like marbles, and you could always SPOT someone who had a LARGE stone collection from the way they carried their school bag.

In class Marcus kept showing me and AMY what he thought was a really interesting stone.

"What do you think this one looks like?" he asked.

"A stone," I answered.

"You know what I mean.

What do you think it is, AMY?"

"Give me a clue."

"Isn't it OBVIOUS?"

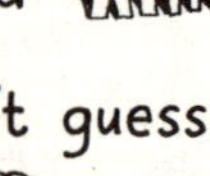

"Errr, not really," AMY and I told Marcus.

I didn't know and neither did AMY.

Marcus got annoyed that we couldn't guess it.

"It's an AARDVARK*, of course!"

"What does an AARDVARK look like?"

I asked, and Marcus showed me the stone again.

"Like THIS!" he said.

"Like a STONE?"

"Oh, never mind..."

*See page 224 for an aardvark picture!

Here's a chart I made of the BEST stones to find.

The only STONE I was missing to complete my stone with a HOLE collection was a BIG one.

Derek and I had been looking for AGES, but we hadn't managed to find the EXACT-size stone with a hole in.

THEN Mr Fullerman announced we were all going on a SCHOOL TRIP. He said we'd all be taking part in ⇨ **Pick Up Plastic Week** and going to a LAKE!

This was EXCITING NEWS for lots of different reasons (mostly because LAKES = LOADS OF STONES).

I'd be able to find EXACTLY the right stone. It would be so much easier by a LAKE, wouldn't it?

(YES.)

happy face

The stone craze in school was still going on, so I knew that stone competition would be FIERCE.

BUT I wasn't going to worry about it.

Hopefully there would be enough to go around.

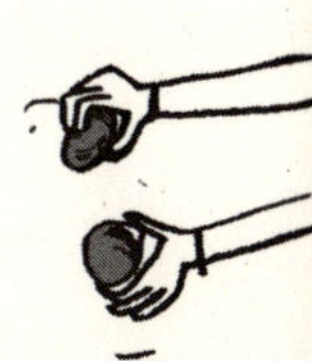

On the day of the school **Pick Up Plastic Week** trip, I was a bit late (Uh-oh!) because I'd spent too long trying to decide which STONES I should bring with me. I needed to compare sizes and find the PERFECT stone to add to my collection. Just to be on the safe side I brought a few in my bag to compare.

"Your bag looks **heavy**, Tom. What have you got in there?" Dad asked.

"All the important stuff for the trip," I told him.

Dad gave me a lift to school so I didn't miss the coach. I was the last kid to arrive, running with my heavy bag.

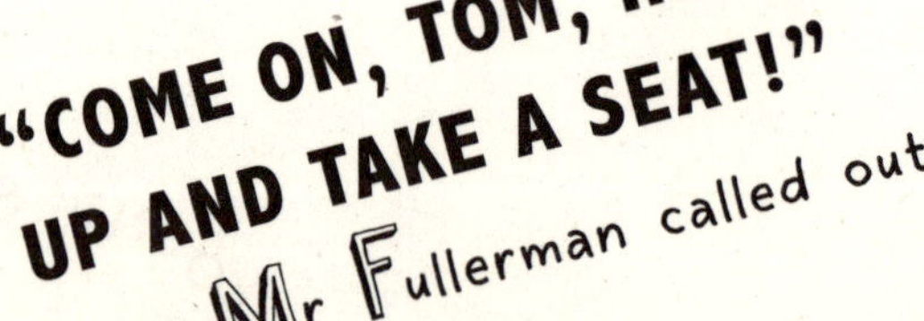

"COME ON, TOM, HURRY UP AND TAKE A SEAT!" Mr Fullerman called out.

Normally Derek would have saved me a seat next to him, but his class are doing this trip on a different day. The only seat left was next to ...

... Julia Morton.

She was already holding a sick bag.

"This is for EMERGENCY only, Tom. I'm much better at travelling now," Julia assured me. Once the coach set off, Julia was fine.

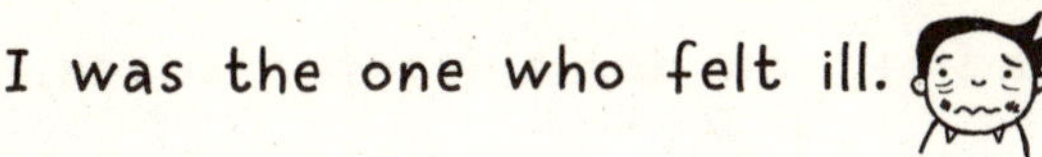

I was the one who felt ill.

All that swerving around and STOP ...

START was making me feel properly QUEASY.

"Here, take this..." Julia handed me the bag.

It wasn't a good start to the trip.

I managed to hold it together until we arrived at the lake and got off the coach. (Phew!)

Mr Fullerman saw the colour of my face and asked, **"Are you OK, Tom? Take some deep breaths of FRESH AIR and you'll feel better."**

So I did.

It was working until Norman offered me one of his **PICKLED ONION** snacks.

Normally I'd LOVE one, but the smell wasn't helping.

"You must feel bad if you don't want a snack," Norman noted.

"I'll be fine," I said and breathed some more.

Mr Fullerman gathered us all around and said, **"Isn't it great, Class 5F, to be by the lake in the lovely fresh air and SUN."**

Just then it started to rain ... a LOT.

I looked around at all my classmates who were wearing waterproof coats and were nice and dry – not like me.

"You <u>did</u> bring SOMETHING WATERPROOF to wear, didn't you, Tom?"

Mr Fullerman asked.

"Not really..." I said.

Holding a piece of paper over my head wasn't working.

Mrs Mumble came to my rescue with the spare clothes bag.

"I don't have a coat, Tom, but I'll see what else we can find for you."

Mrs Mumble brought out what looked like a blanket and a small umbrella.

"It's not ideal; the blanket is for picnics, but it's waterproof and will keep you dry," she told me.

"And this might work too," she added.

Mrs Mumble put the blanket round my shoulders like a cloak and then opened up a really small umbrella and put it ... ON MY HEAD LIKE A HAT!

"It's better than getting soaking wet, Tom," she told me, as the rain bounced off the umbrella hat.

Marcus made a special effort to come over and tell me,

"At least I'm keeping DRY,"

I replied.

Which was true until Norman jumped in a puddle and my legs got soaking wet.

"Sorry, Tom. Nice umbrella hat, though," Norman said.

Mr Fullerman took us to meet the **Pick Up Plastic Week** crew who were waiting for us under a shelter.

"HELLO, Class 5F from Oakfield School. We are so happy you've joined us today to be part of our **Pick Up Plastic** campaign," the lady said cheerily. "My name is YELLOW. Before you ask, that IS my real name."

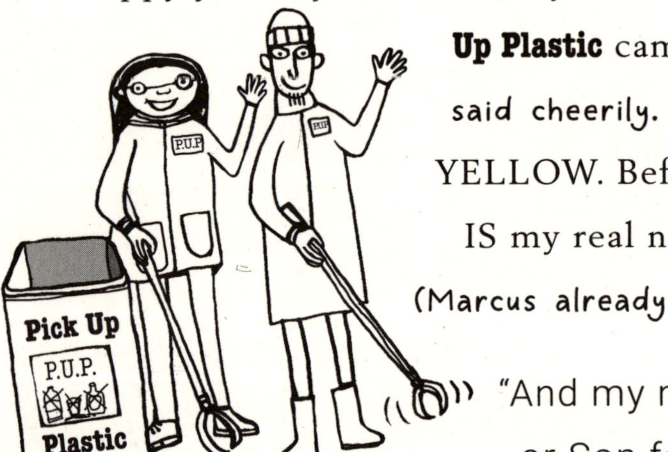

(Marcus already had his hand up.)

"And my name is SONNY, or Son for short.

So together we're Yellow and Son."

They both waved at us enthusiastically.

We waved back just as enthusiastically.

"Today you'll be helping us to collect any rubbish – particularly PLASTIC – from around the lake to keep it clean," Sonny said. He demonstrated how we could use TONGS to pick up the plastic.

"We'll give you gloves and you should use the tongs for anything you want to pick up," Yellow said. "Don't use your hands and make sure you wear the gloves. Put all the plastic in these bins."

"We can all do that, can't we, Class 5F?"

Mr Fullerman aked.

"YES!"

We were excited.

None of us could WAIT to try out the tongs ...

... **On** each other.

Mr Fullerman put a stop to our fun with his

STARE OF DOOM.

"Everyone, follow Yellow and Sonny to the lake, please," he said firmly.

"Tom, hurry up. You don't need your bag."

(I <u>did</u> need a stone from my bag to help me find the **PERFECT** sized stone for my collection, so I grabbed one and put it in my pocket.)

Marcus (nosy parker) wanted to know why I was bringing a stone with me.

"I'm looking for the next size up from this stone to complete my collection," I said. "A lake is a good place for that."

"You're SUPPOSED to be looking for plastic, not stones, Tom," Marcus told me (smugly).

"I can do both." I smiled.

But as we got closer to the water, I could see my stone-collecting plans might not be so easy.

"Oh dear, Tom, not many stones on all this **grass**. Bad luck," Marcus enjoyed telling me.

I was going to try even harder now.

With our tongs at the ready, my class set off in the rain to clear up any plastic or rubbish from the (VERY) grassy and non-stony lake.

It wasn't long before I was expertly picking up bottle tops, torn plastic bags, lolly sticks and a few other bits and pieces.

It felt good to be doing something useful.

All the time, though, I kept my eyes OPEN for excellent stones.

I was starting to think this was going to be impossible when

SOMETHING CAUGHT MY EYE.

It might be a stone. It was slightly hidden under some weeds, so I moved closer for a better LOOK and noticed the stone was SPARKLING.

Could it be?

Was it?

Stone number **two** on my list.

A stone with a CRYSTAL in it.

This was EXCITING!

I didn't want to bring too much attention to the stone. I tried to *relax* and casually move nearer with my TONGS at the ready to pick it up.

When a GUST OF WIND WHISKED THE UMBRELLA HAT OFF MY **HEAD.**

I chased it along the ground and grabbed it with my tongs. Then I put it back on quickly.

AGH!

By the time I got back to MY stone ...

... it had **GONE** and ...

(Oh.)

AMY was holding it.

"Look at this stone I found, Tom. It's AMAZING. It was just under that bit of weed. I've always wanted a stone like this."

"Yeah ... me too." I sighed.

"I can't believe I saw it sparkling. I never thought stones were that interesting until I saw your collection," AMY said.

I tried to be pleased for her.

"I can't believe you saw it either."

Marcus came over to have a look.

"Did you find that stone, Tom?"

"No, I did," AMY replied.

"Bad luck, Tom," Marcus said.

"I'm going to keep looking. There MUST be more stones by this lake," I told Marcus.

"Good idea. I want to find a stone like that too."

I pretended not to care that Marcus wanted to join in.

(But I did.)

Mr Fullerman pointed to the ground, which was code for **"get back to picking up plastic".**

"Look, sir, I've found a stone with a crystal in it!" AMY said and everyone gathered round to see the glittery stone.

"EXCELLENT, Amy. You're all doing a fantastic job. Keep it up!"

I decided to go in a different direction to Marcus, and was determined NOT to get distracted by anything this time. I was going to find my PERFECT STONE.

Using my tongs, I looked under weeds, checked behind rocks and kept my eyes peeled.

Solid came over to join me. He was holding a plastic bottle to put in the bin.

"I like using these tongs, don't you?" he asked.

"Yes! Although I'm trying to find interesting stones for my collection as well. I haven't found anything yet. It's not <u>that</u> easy by a lake, is it?" I said to Solid.

"I don't know, Tom. Look what I found over there." Solid took a flat stone from his pocket ...

... with what looked like a **FOSSIL** inside.

"I've never found anything like this before. It's great, isn't it?" Solid said.

I WAS (ALMOST) SPEECHLESS!

Yes, it is... That looks like a **FOSSIL** in the stone, Solid.

"I thought so. I'm going to add it to my collection. I only started collecting stones after your show and tell. Thanks, Tom."

"No problem, Solid." I sighed.

"Where did you find it again?" I asked.

"Over there, just where Marcus is standing," Solid told me. (Brilliant.)

Should I go over and join Marcus, or look in another place?

Finding a **FOSSIL** would be AMAZING. I took a risk.

And I joined Marcus.

As SOON as he saw me, he said,

"Solid found a stone with a **FOSSIL** in it."

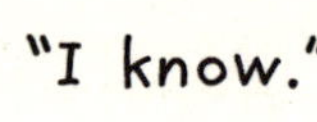

"I know."

"That's what I'm looking for," he added.

"Me too."

We both got busy trying to find anything that resembled a stone. Marcus wasn't going to get one before me, not this time. But it wasn't easy. We got in each other's way picking up what we both thought were stones.

"I saw it first..." I told him.

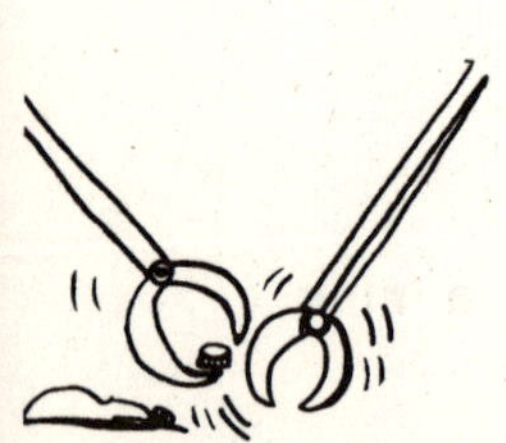

"HEY, that was mine..."

Marcus kept saying,

which was annoying.

I let Marcus take what I could see was a bottle top. I'd spotted something right by his foot that looked VERY promising. I glanced down quickly and could see it was a STONE! Not just any old stone, but what looked like the EXACT SIZE I needed to complete my COLLECTION!

While Marcus kept on talking about Solid's **FOSSIL**, I tried my best to move my tongs closer to the stone without Marcus noticing. Slowly ... slowly ... slowly... Until Marcus only went and STOOD right on top of the stone.

"What's that?" he said and lifted his foot up to take a look.

"It's NOTHING!" I shouted.

"Doesn't look like nothing to me..."

"HEY! It's my LUCKY DAY. Look, Tom, I've found this STONE with a hole. I've started collecting these stones since your show and tell. It's not a **FOSSIL**, but I'm going to KEEP IT,"

Marcus told me excitedly.

Awww no!

"That's EXACTLY the size of stone I was looking for," I said, hoping Marcus might give it to me.

(No chance.)

Marcus enjoyed waving the stone out of my reach.

"I wouldn't do that if I were you," I said.

"It's MY stone now." Marcus LAUGHED. He knew I collected those stones.

"Marcus, there's a seagull flying towards you and it thinks you've got FOOD," I tried to explain.

"Yeah, right, Tom. Like I'm going to fall for that," he said smugly before...

The seagull swooped down and grabbed the stone and flew off.

Marcus yelped,

"**AGH!** That's MINE! Mr Fullerman, a seagull took my STONE!" he yelped.

Marcus was so busy shouting and running away that he didn't see the seagull DROP the stone out of its mouth.

BUT I did... And I saw where it landed too. I quickly picked up the stone and kept it safely under my blanket. The rain even stopped and the sun came out.

Things were really looking up for me.

"But was the seagull OK?" Mr Fullerman checked. He didn't seem that worried about Marcus.

"It was the biggest seagull ever," Marcus exaggerated.

"SIR?"

It was time for us to stop collecting, and Sonny and Yellow congratulated everyone on all our hard work. "Great job, Oakfield School, you've all worked so hard collecting up the rubbish and plastic."

I was thinking.

Mrs Mumble took back my umbrella hat and blanket, which was pretty wet.

"Wasn't it useful? I might get one for myself," she said.

I popped my NEW stone with a hole into my bag before Marcus saw it. I was looking forward to getting home and adding it to my collection.

I wasn't the only one.

"I'm so HAPPY I found this crystal stone!" AMY told the class as we ate our packed lunches.

"My **FOSSIL** stone is the BEST thing I've EVER found!" Solid said.

"SIR, did I tell you my stone with a hole in got pinched by a bird?" Marcus wanted to SHARE.

"You did, Marcus." Mr Fullerman sighed.

"Your class are very into collecting things," Yellow noted.

"I think it's a school trend. It's stones this week and pencil rubbers the next!" Mr Fullerman explained. (He could be right.) Sitting next to Julia on the coach back home, she did have a pencil with an excellent face on a rubber at the end. (I could collect them!)

The first thing I did when I got home was to get out all my stones with holes and arrange them in size order. My new stone fit in perfectly and looking at the stone's shape, it really reminded me of something.

I used my special pen and drew a face on the stone. Now it will ALWAYS remind me of going on the **Pick Up Plastic** school trip and all the funny things that happened.

Here is Marcus Meldrew when he ignored my warning and the bird pinched his stone.

Looking at my stone makes me LAUGH. Ha! Ha! Ha! Ha! Ha! Ha! Ha! Ha! Ha! Ha! Ha! Ha!

I hope Mr Fullerman will find it funny and ★★★★★ immediately give me FIVE STARS for this story.

Or I could write about my EMPTY box of

Chocteezers.

I know it doesn't look like much, but they are one of my FAVOURITE treats to have in the cinema. They are chocolate on the outside and caramel on the inside. I wish I had some now.

Here's the story of why I kept this empty box of **Chocteezers**.

My Five-Star Funny Story
The mystery of the Chocteezers
lovely chocolatey smell
Chocteezers
Chocteezers
by Tom Gates
HA! HA!
HA! HA!

I got THIS BOX at the CINEMA CLUB with Derek and my friends.

Derek had to remind me we were going with a BIG sign at his bedroom window that said

Then he followed it up with this sign about jelly snakes.

I gave him the thumbs up and wrote a quick sign myself.

Leroy and Norman were meeting us at the CINEMA with DIFFERENT snacks, so the sooner we got there the BETTER.

Leroy was bringing **cheese puffs**, Derek had jelly snakes and Norman wasn't sure what he was bringing. He was going to decide on the day.

One of my favourite things about going to the CINEMA is getting a box of **Chocteezers** as a treat. ☺

I'd promised my friends that I'd SHARE them.

(Not the WHOLE box – they'd understand.)

Derek was so quick to come round that I wasn't ready, and Delia got to the door before me.

Derek said, still swinging jelly snakes from his head.

"Really? I'd never have guessed," Delia told him with a straight face.

"The snakes suit you," Delia said.

I came to his rescue just in time.

"YES! JELLY SNAKES! Can I have one now?"

Derek passed one over.

"That's been in Derek's hair, Tom!"

Delia told me like that was a problem.

"They weren't IN my hair, I was just holding them near it," Derek said.

He offered Delia a snake as well.

"Want one?"

Ewwwwww.

It was nice of him, but Delia wasn't keen.

I ate my snake like it was a piece of spaghetti, holding it above my mouth and dropping it down.

(The first of many treats that day ... mmmm.)

Dad was in the kitchen and asked what film we were going to see.

SWAMP MONSTER 3.

We told him in our best **MONSTER** voices.

"I might come and see it with you. That sounds like FUN!" Dad said.

NO! You can't!

I answered a bit too fast. We'd planned to go to the **CINEMA CLUB** with just our friends (and snacks), not with Dad.

"You could give us a lift though, so we're not late?" I added.

Dad LAUGHED. "I suppose I could."

"And maybe buy us some drinks and a box of **Chocteezers?"**

I thought it was worth asking.

Derek gave him a jelly snake so he didn't feel bad.

Dad ate the jelly snake and took us to the cinema EARLY so we could get the GOOD seats.

The kids' club is ALWAYS popular and SWAMP MONSTER 3 was a film LOADS of kids wanted to see.

It was already packed when we arrived. Dad signed us in, and we put on our wristbands.

"You two go and join the queue and I'll get some drinks for you," Dad told us.

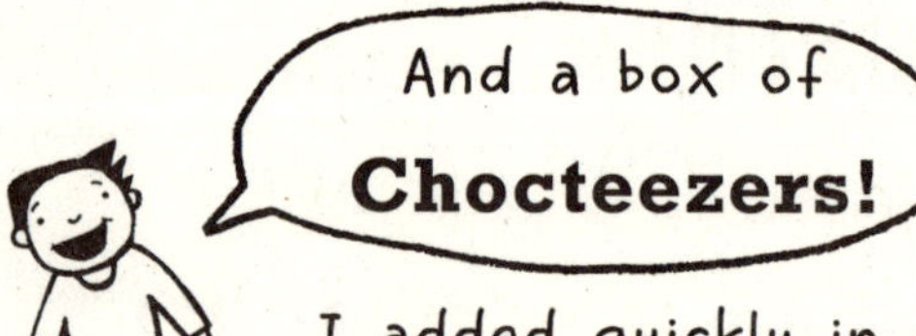

I added quickly in case he'd forgotten.

"YOU'LL NEVER GUESS WHO'S AT THE FRONT OF THE QUEUE!"

Derek said, sounding excited.

"Not Marcus...?" I sighed.

It was ONLY LEROY AND Norman!

They were standing right next to the cinema entrance, which was IMPRESSIVE. We'd all be first inside now!

We ran over to join them and let the other kids in the queue know we WEREN'T pushing in. (No one likes a pusher in.)

"Nice work, guys, now we can all get seats together," I said happily.

We compared snacks while waiting for Dad and worked out how to divide them up.

Norman had brought toast in a lunch box. (Random.)

"It's got chocolate spread on it, cut into fingers so we can share it," he said, which made sense.

Then I heard one of my FAVOURITE sounds EVER...

rattle
rattle

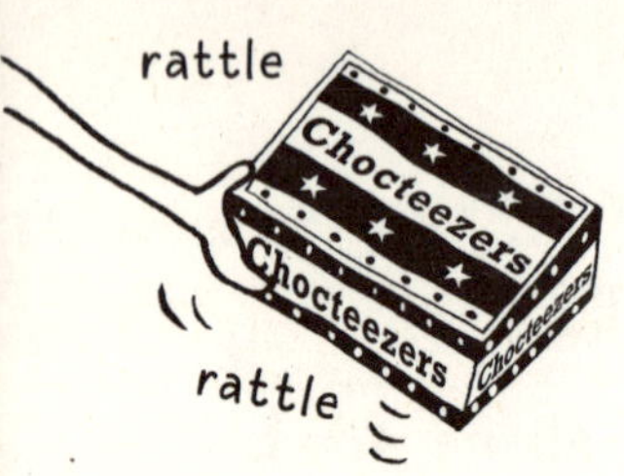

A FULL BOX OF CHOCTEEZERS.

I could tell Norman was rethinking his toast.

"Don't panic... I'll share them," I assured him.

(Not the WHOLE box, obviously.)

Dad passed me the **Chocteezers** and gave Norman and Leroy their drinks.

"Are you staying for the film, Mr Gates?" Leroy asked.

"I could do," Dad said, surprising me. "But I won't. Enjoy the film. Behave, Tom, and I'll meet you all here after."

"And don't forget ...

I'LL BE BACK!"

(He said this in a very deep, very loud voice.)

"Thanks, Dad," I said and waved him goodbye (before he did THAT voice again).

"Does your dad always talk like that?" asked Leroy.

"Only in front of my friends."

I noticed Leroy had brought a LARGE bag with him – that looked promising.

"I've got **cheese puffs.** One bag for each of us," he said. "And a cushion in case someone tall sits in front of me."

(Leroy had thought of everything.)

"We should PLAN where we're going to sit before we go in," Derek suggested.

"We can sit ANYWHERE we want to – we're FIRST in the QUEUE!" Norman reminded us.

We had a BIG chat about all the BEST places to sit. Norman likes being in the middle, Derek at the back, Leroy thought four seats at the side would be good, and I like sitting at the front. We were so busy talking that we didn't notice the queue had started to move ...

IN THE OTHER DIRECTION.

This was a DISASTER.

We'd been standing at the WRONG DOOR and now we were right at the BACK and all the good seats would be gone!

"Come on! Let's just go to the front," Derek suggested.

But when we got there, the kids' club lady told us to wait in line.

"There's no hurry, you'll all get in. It's a BIG CINEMA," she said.

Yeah, NO pushing in! someone in the queue shouted. (Marcus Meldrew.)

"We were here FIRST – at the wrong door!" I tried to explain.

But it was no good. We had to go all the way to the BACK, walking past AMY, Florence and Marcus, who waved.

"You should have got here earlier." He smiled.

It was very annoying. Derek was FUMING, so to lighten the mood I opened the **Chocteezers** and offered them round (which helped).

At least the queue moved pretty fast and it didn't take long to get to the front, where we showed our wristbands and went inside. Only to find all the good seats were GONE. The whole cinema was FULL and trying to find FOUR seats all together was looking impossible.

"Are we going to have to sit separately and not share our snacks?" Leroy asked.

"No! Let's keep looking," I said.

Then Norman shouted,

"OVER THERE!"

and pointed to FOUR SEATS one row back from the front. We ran as fast as we could and grabbed them before anyone sat there.

I even had two spare seats next to me.

Things were looking UP. ☺

Until the TALLEST grown-up sat in front of Leroy. He just reached into his bag, got out the cushion, and was instantly LIFTED UP (like magic!).

Cushions rule... Leroy said.

(I had cushion envy as Leroy looked EXTRA comfy too.)

Before the film started, we got settled and shared out the snacks. I passed my **Chocteezers** down so everyone could take some and I tried not to JUDGE when Norman took quite a lot.

Huh?

Then I carefully put my box on the EMPTY SEAT next to me. Waiting for the film to start, I had a few cheese puffs before the adverts finished and the lights went down ...

... when two latecomers sat in the empty seats next to me RIGHT ON MY **Chocteezers**.

I had a moment of **PANIC** before I spotted them on the arm rest between the seats. It was a HUGE relief, until I heard the NOISE of my **Chocteezers** moving around.

Someone was TAKING them!

This was a VERY **BAD** situation that I needed to STOP right away. I reached down to take MY **Chocteezers** back, but the kid next to me was already holding them. They took my **Chocteezers** and ...

OPENED them!

I was just about to SHOUT OUT:

"HEY! Those are MINE!"

when I heard the kid say:

Chocteezers are the BEST.

I FROZE. I recognized that voice. Of ALL the kids to sit next to me, why did it have to be

BUSTER JONES?

He was always getting in trouble at school.

WHAT was I going to do? Most of the time it was best to AVOID **Buster** or you'd end up in detention.

Avoiding him now was going to be IMPOSSIBLE! I whispered to Derek, "**Buster Jones** is sitting

next to me, and he's taken my **Chocteezers.**"

Derek gulped, leaned forwards, then back.

"Don't make eye contact. He doesn't know it's you," Derek told me, and passed the message on to

Leroy and Norman, who also took a sneaky peek. Norman passed me some of his chocolate-spread toast.

"Norman says you should eat this instead – to avoid any trouble," Derek said.

It was good advice.

No one liked standing up to **Buster Jones.**

But these were MY **Chocteezers,** and it wasn't FAIR.

I took a deep breath ... and slowly, quietly, began to put my hand into the box.

The **Chocteezers** kept rolling around and were very noisy. But I managed to eat a handful without **Buster** noticing.

(I'd just SHOW him they were mine.)

Buster picked the box up and passed it to his friend.

"Help yourself," I heard him say...

(Oh no...)

THIS IS A DISASTER!

Buster's friend was eating them now. I didn't want to get on the WRONG side of **Buster** (or his friend). I tried to concentrate on the film, but all I could hear were my **Chocteezers** being eaten ...

... and not by me.

I just had to sit quietly until **Buster** put my box back on the armrest. I took my chance and tried to eat some more before they were all gone. The box was nearly EMPTY. I had to be BRAVE and pluck up the courage to tell **Buster** to stop eating my **Chocteezers!**

I decided to wait for the right time to say something.

I waited ...

and waited ...

(ate some toast) 

and then waited some more.

Just as the film finished and the credits began to roll, I took a deep breath.

Derek nudged me.

"Good film, wasn't it?" he asked.

"I wouldn't know. It was hard to FOCUS," I whispered, pointing in **Buster's** direction. "I'm going to tell him they were mine," I added.

"That's going to be hard," Derek said.

"I know but I HAVE to say something..."

"**No,** you can't..."

"Why Not?"

"Because he's already gone!" Derek said.

I turned around and sure enough, **Buster** and his friend had left, leaving behind my VERY empty **Chocteezers** box. I'd missed out on EVERYTHING: the film AND my treats.

I picked up the empty box and showed it to Norman, Leroy and Derek.

"Sorry about the **Chocteezers**, Tom. Here, have the last piece of chocolate-spread toast," Norman said, but the toast looked a bit squashed so I didn't take it. Dad would be waiting outside, so we began to make our way past the other seats when my foot touched something on the floor.

I bent down to take a look only to find...

Chocteezers
Chocteezers
A FULL BOX OF Chocteezers.
(My full box of Chocteezers...)

The box that **Buster** <u>must</u> have moved when he sat down. I suddenly realized I'd been helping myself to **Buster Jones's** **Chocteezers** the WHOLE TIME. Sneaking handfuls whenever I could.

I shuddered and tried not to think about what **Buster Jones** would have done if he'd caught me.

I was just very happy to find my treats.

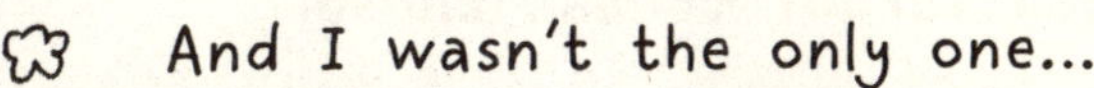

And I wasn't the only one...

Leroy, Derek and Norman were SUPER happy I'd found another box! The sound of them rattling wasn't as loud as Dad's monster voice calling out:

"HOW WAS SWAMP MONSTER 3? DID YOU ENJOY THE FILM?"

"It was AMAZING, Mr Gates ... especially the SONGS!" Leroy told him.

"I missed the songs," I whispered.

"I can't believe you've still got a WHOLE box of **Chocteezers**, Tom. It must have been a really good film if you forgot to eat those!"

Dad LAUGHED.

"I might have to watch it again," I told him.

In the car going home, I shared the **Chocteezers** out.

By the time we'd dropped off

Norman ...

Leroy ...

and Derek ...

the **Chocteezers** were (nearly) all gone.

I managed to eat the last few before Delia saw them.

And the lovely smell of chocolate has STAYED in the box for a very long time.

Every now and then I like to pick up the box and remember when it was filled with **Chocteezers** in the cinema, while trying hard to forget about **Buster Jones.**

(I still haven't seen **SWAMP MONSTER 3**, though!)

I spent a bit of time doodling on the empty box lid with my special pen.

It looks even nicer now.

If I got ★★★★★ for this story, I would celebrate with some **Chocteezers**

(obviously).

I **STILL** can't decide what I should write about to get into the FIRST EVER Oakfield School book of FUNNY STORIES.

Even the pen I'm holding has a FUNNY STORY behind it. Granny Mavis bought it for me. It's the BEST pen in the **WHOLE WIDE WORLD.**

(Really!)

It writes on most things like paper, wood, shoes, my pencil case, stones and other things too.

Dad's hat

Here's the story of how I got my special pen...

My Five-Star Funny Story
special pen
fancy lines
my special pen
by
Tom Gates
HA! HA!
HA! HA!

When I am very old (like THE FOSSILS), I will STILL be using my special pen to draw on things (hopefully).

I'm trying **hard** not to lose it because I can be a bit forgetful.

One trick I have is to TIE a piece of string to my pen. When Marcus Meldrew TOOK it, he got a bit of a **SURPRISE**. I pulled the string and pinged the pen right back into my hands.

This may seem a bit **EXTREME**, but it does stop stuff from going missing.

Mum likes to pretend she NEVER loses things, but I know she does.

Once she bought a book about how to be organized and tidy.

"This book is going to

CHANGE OUR LIVES.

We all need to be more

tidy in this house."

Then she put the book down somewhere and lost it. Mum looked everywhere. Eventually, I was the one who found it under a big pile of magazines. →

"I think you need this book more than I do..." I said.

"I wondered where that went!"

Dad loved telling ANYONE who'd listen how Mum had lost the tidy book.

Dad loses things too.

Once I saw him on his phone talking to Mum.

Rita, do you know where my phone is?

I can't find it.

All the time it was in his hand...

Mum likes telling THAT story.

Delia loses things as well...

She likes to blame ME when her sunglasses go missing.

(I admit sometimes I borrow them, but not always.)

Like the time they were on her head.

"Because they're on your head," I told her.

Granny Mavis is VERY organized and doesn't often lose things.

(She always knows where Granddad has left his teeth.)

Here!

Once Granny came to see us on her roller skates. She was on the way to buy some new glasses and wondered if I wanted to come with her.

Wheeeee!

"I need to get some NEW frames and I can't see what they look like. Could you help me, Tom?" she asked.

Of course I said YES!

Granny Mavis is ALWAYS fun to hang out with.

"It will be lovely to have your company, Tom," Granny told me.

I took my mini scooter to try and keep up with Granny on her skates.

(She has a LOT of energy.)

We got to the opticians in no time at all.

It was easy to see the sign outside that said:

GREAT exSPECStations.

Granny took off her skates and I left my scooter in a safe place by the door.

Then I followed her into the HUGE shop to help choose some fancy new glasses.

Inside I'd never seen **SO MANY** pairs of glasses. There were **FRAMES** of all different shapes and sizes. Rows and rows and rows of them.

"Right, Tom, let's get started. I need you to say if they suit me. I can't see a thing without my **REAL** glasses," Granny explained.

"OK, Granny," I said, then I tried her glasses on for fun. Everything looked **BLURRY** so I took them off.

Granny was already wearing a pair of **BIG** round frames.

"How about these, Tom?" she asked.

"They make you look like a rockstar, Granny."

"Excellent, let's keep them." She **LAUGHED**.

Granny spent a really long time trying on EVERY kind of shape of glasses you could imagine. Square shaped, star glasses, oval, wobbly frames, until finally ...

... she found a pair she liked.

"I like these, Tom. Let's get them. Now where did you put my REAL glasses?" Granny asked me.

It was a VERY good question as neither of us could see them. (Especially Granny.)

"They're here somewhere," I muttered.

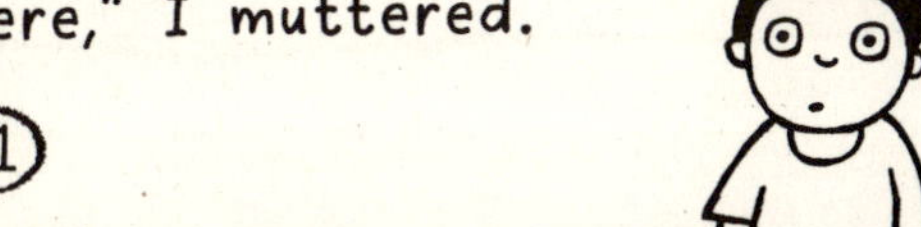

"Oh no, Tom, you haven't?" Granny said.

(I had...)

They could be ANYWHERE in the shop.

We walked UP and DOWN, tracing our steps back and looking on EVERY shelf. "It's not good, Tom. This is going to take forever." Granny sighed. Then I spotted a lady trying on what looked like Granny's glasses and admiring her reflection in a mirror.

"These lovely OLD vintage glasses are JUST what I've been looking for. They're PERFECT. I'll take them!" she said.

"I think I found them, Granny!" I said and rushed over to explain that the glasses weren't for sale. "I'm sorry. Those belong to my granny. She's over there waving at you," I told the lady, who was very nice and waved back. "She can't see you because you're wearing her glasses," I pointed out.

Granny was super grateful, and we had a good **LAUGH** about her glasses once she got them back.

"Now I know how your granddad feels when he loses his teeth," she told me.

(That's happened a few times before.) ☺

Once Granny had ordered her new glasses, we decided to walk back to her house. Granny said she'd had enough excitement for one day.

"I've got another job for you, Tom," she told me.

"Oh... OK," I said. BUT, even though I like helping THE FOSSILS, the word JOB made me think it wouldn't be much fun.

So when we got back to the house and Granny gave me the special PEN,

I was EXCITED.

"You can decorate the ends of my glasses so I'll always be able to SPOT them in the shop," she told me.

(DREAM JOB!)

I decorated the ends of Granny's glasses with my EXPERT doodles.

And her glasses case too.

"Now, Tom ...

even though this pen draws on loads of different things, always ask permission before you draw on anything. You don't want to get into trouble,"

Granny reminded me.

"Yes, Granny."

I did TRY and remember that ...

... most of the time.

(The stars came
off eventually...)

Delia doesn't love my special pen as much as I do. When I was younger, **she** used to tell <u>me</u> stories.

Then I'd tell THOSE stories to my friends and discover THEY WEREN'T TRUE.

"Did Delia tell you that?" Derek would say. Now I'm older, I'm not fooled by her NONSENSE.

Here are Delia's top four made-up stories:

- Eating the crusts on your bread will make your hair curly.

- If you eat FRUIT with pips, the pips will grow in your tummy and out of your ears.

- Delia said she had special powers and could talk to animals.

- Cabbage makes you taller.

After a **long** time staring at all my stuff and thinking about the stories that go with them: *Great-Aunt Aggie's Hat,* my stone with a hole, the empty **Chocteezers** box, my special pen, I know what I'm going to write about.

I can't get distracted by ANYTHING or I'll be late handing it in, and then I won't get

FIVE STARS.

Here goes...

(Just doing my five-star doodle first.)

Five-star distraction bugs. ↑

I finished my story and handed it in ON TIME (result!).

AMY asks me what I wrote about.

"Something FUNNY, I hope!" I tell her.

"I wrote a FUNNY poem," AMY says.

"Isn't it supposed to be a STORY?" Marcus joins in.

"Mr Fullerman said a poem's OK too. It's a FUNNY poem, so I hope it gets into the book. It's about socks," AMY tells us.

"My story is VERY FUNNY. I wrote about something that happened to me,"

Marcus says very confidently.

"So did I," I say.

I wonder what stories will make it into

Oakfield School's first ever

FIVE-STAR STORY BOOK.

(Not long to wait.)

random bat

"Well done, EVERYONE! You should be very proud of yourselves. AND even if you're not in THIS book, you'll get a special certificate, a badge and a smiley face sticker,"

Mr Fullerman said.

(He's in a VERY good mood.)

"I enjoyed reading ALL your poems and stories. I've learnt about what makes you laugh and I had a lot of LAUGHS myself. It won't be long before you'll be able to read Oakfield School's **first EVER book of FIVE-STAR STORIES."**

Sir! Sir! Did you like my cheese and dragons story?

"I liked all the stories, Norman."

Finally! Here's my copy.

I put a sticker
on it so everyone knows
it's mine.

Oakfield School Five-Star Stories
Oakfield School
Five-Star
Stories
Volume 1
★★★★★
Stories, poems and
other funny stuff by
the pupils of
Oakfield School
Tom Gates

This book belongs to:
Tom Gates
(because I got 5 stars!)
Welcome to the first ever
FUNNY FIVE-STAR STORIES book.
Congratulations to everyone who took part.
If you got five stars for your work, WELL DONE!
We hope it encourages you to keep on
writing your funny stories and poems
so we can make another book.

Oakfield School
Five-Star Stories
By the pupils of
Oakfield School
I added
a bug!
Published by
Oakfield School

Here's Florence Mitchell trying not to laugh while singing **"The Silly Song of Sounds"** with her band **Florence and the Smiley Faces.**

The Silly Song of Sounds

By Florence Mitchell

(Absolutely NO LAUGHING when you say this.)

Yippy Yappy

Yeah Yeah

Yippy Yappy Yoooo

Fribble Frabble FROO FROO

Wibble Wobble Woo

Hippy Happy HAY HEY

Yippy Yappy YOU!

HIPPY HOPPY

Hoo Hoo

Hippy Happy

Hey!

(Repeat as many times as you can.)

FUN AND NAMES

BY* ...

(This story didn't have a name on it but is being included because Mr Keen has a good idea who it might be and we all enjoyed it.)

Mr Tedious was the head teacher of Snoore School, the most **BORING** school in the whole wide world. ***EVERYTHING*** about the school was **DULL.**

The lessons were MIND-NUMBINGLY boring.

Mr Tedious had the dreariest voice EVER. It sent all the children to sleep.

*Mystery kid who wrote this story.

This was a **HUGE** problem because **Mr Tedious** was also *MEAN* and anyone who didn't stay awake would get a

BIG BORING DETENTION.

The children tried **VERY** hard to pay attention and keep their eyes open.

But it wasn't easy.

Every morning the day would start like this...

Mr Tedious would stand in front of the **WHOLE school** and read out a list of children who'd ***FALLEN ASLEEP*** in lessons.

It was a

and by the time he'd finished reading it, even **MORE** children were ***asleep.***

(Sooo boring.)

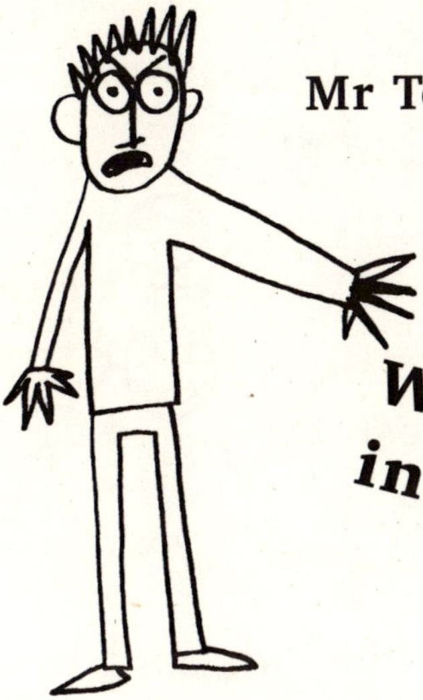

Mr Tedious would ***shout,***

"You there! Stop snoozing! Wake up! You are in detention!"

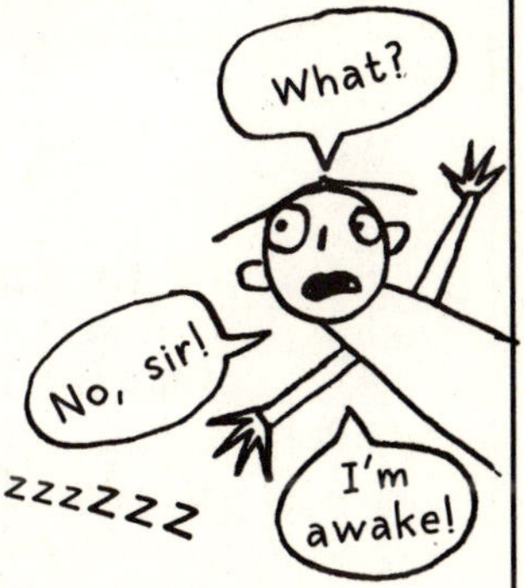
What?
No, sir!
I'm awake!

(This happened EVERY DAY.)

zzzzZZzzzzzzzzZZZzzzZZZZZZZzzzZZZ

Lessons were a snoozefest too. Then one day after a particularly **BORING** lesson, one kid (a hero 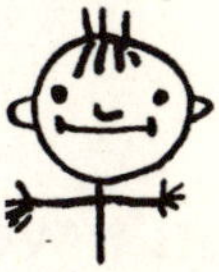 who can't be named for a good reason) said to the other kids that **SOMETHING** had to change.

I have a plan.

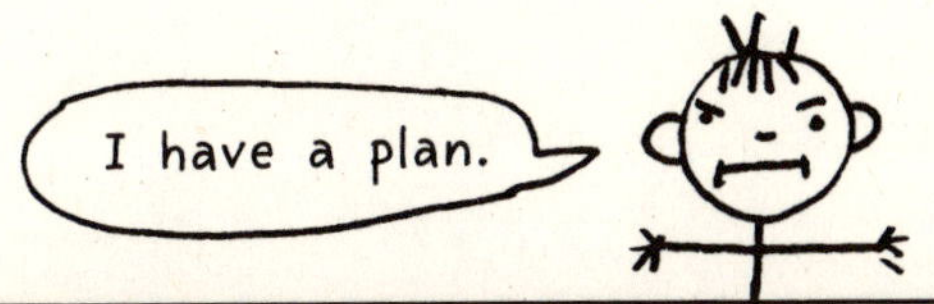

"**Mr Tedious** is SO **DULL** it's impossible to stay **AWAKE** listening to him!"

EVERYONE agreed.

It's true. It's not our fault we can't stay awake. The list is SO BORING!

the other kids said.

"I'm going to **ADD** some **EXTRA** names to the list that will **CHEER** us up, make us ***laugh*** and keep us **awake!"** the kid (who can't be named) told them.

"How are you going to do that?"

the other kids asked.

"I will be **EXTRA** careful, don't worry.

I'm SMART."

The next morning, the kid (who can't be named) ***snuck*** into the school office and CAREFULLY added some **EXTRA** names to **Mr Tedious's** list.

(The kid tried not to ***laugh*** **too much** as the names were making **them giggle.)**

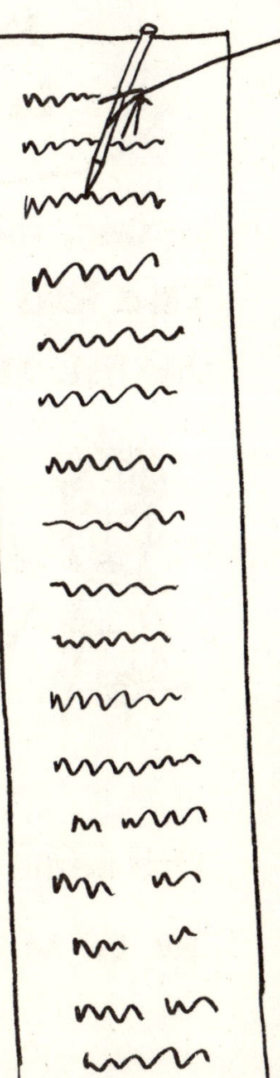

The kid (who can't be named) was really looking forward to school assembly now.

The next day, as he was reading the list, **Mr Tedious** narrowed his eyes and **STARED** at anyone who was making a noise.

Keep quiet or you'll be in detention tomorrow!

he said, then carried on reading.

The kid (who can't be named) was enjoying this list. **Mr Tedious** cleared his throat.

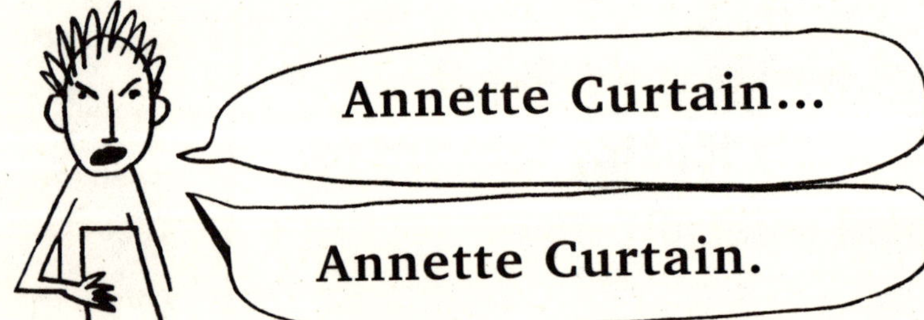

This name also made the children laugh.

He *he* he *he* he *he* he *he* he!

You over there!
Pull yourself together!

Mr Tedious snapped, which only made everyone laugh even more.

Mr Tedious fixed the children with a **stern, BORING** look.

Do you ALL want a detention?

This is NO LAUGHING MATTER.

No one wanted a detention, but this was funny! **The kid** (who can't be named) was trying not to **laugh.**

Mr Tedious waited for silence, then began to read again.

Ben Deelegs...

He! he! he! he! he! he! he!

Ha! ha! ha! ha! ha!

He! he! he! he! he! he! he!

By the time **Mr Tedious** got to the last name on the list ...

... the children thought they would **EXPLODE** into a fit of **giggles** from trying to keep it all inside, including **the kid** (who can't be named).

They were **all** doing **so well** right up until **Mr Tedious** said the **last** child in detention was...

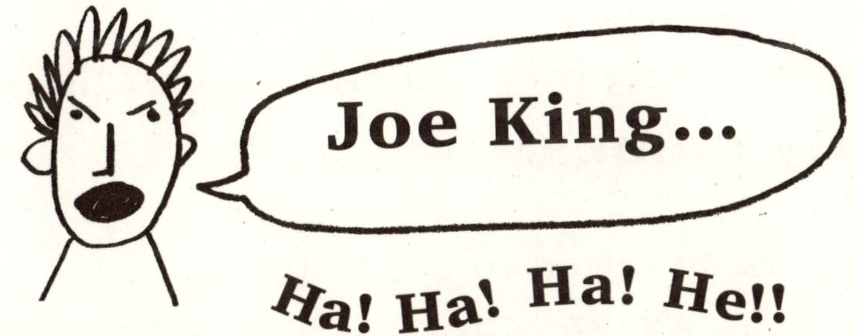

The **whole** school **burst** out *laughing* and couldn't stop for a very long time.

Mr Tedious wasn't happy.

"NO **LAUGHING!**

What **do you** think school is **FOR?**

You're **NOT HERE** to **ENJOY YOURSELVES!"**

he told them.

"You're ALL in

DETENTION!"

The kids didn't care; they couldn't stop laughing at the **silly names**.

Mr Tedious wasn't used to the sound of children having **FUN** and began to ***SLOWLY*** dissolve into a **BIG** puddle of ***DULLNESS.*** No one had to have a **BORING** detention **EVER** again.

The boy (who can't be named) was a hero.

The end.

A poem about my missing sock

By Amy Porter

Where are you, sock?
Where have you gone?
I keep wishing
That you weren't missing
So I could wear
You as a pair.

Answers on page 227.

The VERY Annoying Boys and the **Super Smart Kid**

By Marcus Meldrew

Once upon a time, there were two VERY **annoying** boys who liked to play silly games **ALL** the time.

They enjoyed making people **LOOK** at things that weren't really there.

It was a **RIDICULOUS** game. The boys thought they were SOOOOO clever, but let **ME** tell you – **THEY WERE NOT.**

One day, the boys decided to POINT at the sky and say...

"LOOK, EVERYONE, THERE'S A **SPACESHIP**! DID YOU SEE IT?"

The other children STARED at the sky and believed them, apart from one **smart** kid* who wasn't falling for their **NONSENSE**.

"You haven't seen anything. You're making it up!" the **smart** kid told them.

"We did see something!" the two **annoying** boys said and laughed at ALL the children they had made STARE at nothing.

"If you keep doing that, no one will ever believe you when you DO see something like a **spaceship**."

*Me

The two **annoying** boys didn't care.

"Whatever," they scoffed.

Then one day the **smart** kid looked up at the sky and really **DID** see a **spaceship!**

"Look up at the sky!" he said to the **annoying** boys. "There actually is a **spaceship** this time!"

But the two annoying boys were **TWITS** and **didn't** listen to him.

"Hey! That's OUR game. We're not falling for that," they said.

They IGNORED the **spaceship** that was now **HOVERING OVER THEIR HEADS** (for real).

The **smart** kid watched the spaceship open its door.

"You should look up, it's amazing!" he said, trying to make them take notice.

"Blah, blah, blah...
We know there's nothing there,"
the boys said.

Then a ***LONG*** green **ALIEN** arm came down, scooped them both up and took them away.

"Oh well, I did TRY and warn them," the **smart** kid said and waved them **goodbye.**

He had a nice ***peaceful*** afternoon until the **ALIENS** dropped the two annoying boys back down to earth, because even the **ALIENS** found them **ANNOYING.**

(And the **smart** boy lived happily ever after.)

This is not a story, but a collection of WORDS.
FUNNY WORDS that Make Me Laugh
By Julia Morton
Ha!
Ha!
Ha!
Ha!
Ha!
Ha!
Ha!
Kerfuffle
A disturbance or a bit of a fuss going on.
DOLLOP
Shapeless blob of something – like cream.
Ha!
Wobble
To move unsteadily (or when you're angry or upset).
NITWIT
A silly or foolish person.
Ha!
Ha!
Ha!
Gobbledygook
Language that is meaningless and not easy to understand.
Bumfuzzle
When you're a bit confused or bewildered (or both).
Ha!
Ha!
Ha!

The Dragon and the Cheese

By Norman Watson

Once upon a time, there was a town that made the BIGGEST and most delicious cheese in the whole wide world.

Everyone who lived in the town LOVED cheese. They even had a special

CHEESE PARTY DAY.

People would come from FAR and WIDE to taste the cheese at the party. This year there was GREAT excitement as the CHEESE looked even more delicious.

But the smell of the cheese had attracted attention from a

who decided to FLY into the town and join in the FUN at the party. The dragon had never tasted cheese before.

"It's good to try new things," the dragon said.

The people of the town didn't agree.

They saw the DRAGON looming

towards their GIANT CHEESE

and shouted,

"BACK AWAY FROM

THE GIANT CHEESE. IT'S OURS!"

The dragon didn't like being told what to do

and got the HUMP. It had a bad temper

and began to ...

EVERYWHERE!

The DRAGON spoilt the whole cheese party and the townsfolk had to run for cover.

When the fire brigade came to put out the fire, the dragon HUFFED some more and turned all the water into STEAM.

The townsfolk didn't know what to do. Then a smart girl stepped forward with an excellent plan.

"We need a HUGE loaf of bread and lots of CRACKERS," she told everyone. They thought she had lost the

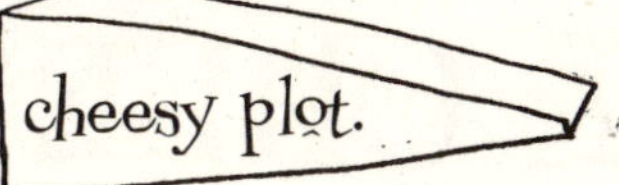

"Trust me, we WILL have a cheesy party and the DRAGON can help us."

(The dragon wasn't so sure.)

The smart girl went to talk to the dragon.

(She was brave as well as smart.)

"Listen up, dragon, we'll let you have some cheese, but you have to be helpful," she said.

The dragon was very hungry and reluctantly decided to help.

Then the little girl asked all the townsfolk to line up their loaves of bread next to the

GIANT CHEESE.

The dragon took a deep breath in and out and the FLAMES that shot out of its mouth toasted the bread and melted the cheese so it bubbled and crisped up, looking even more delicious!

The townsfolk began to tuck in to the toasted bread and melted cheese

and dipped their crackers in too.

The little girl gave some to the dragon, who thought it was DELICIOUS!

Everyone was happy. The girl had found a way to make the cheese party a big success WITH the dragon.

From then on, the townsfolk ALWAYS invited the dragon to the cheese party to toast the bread, melt the cheese and join in with the dancing.

When the little girl wanted to take a photograph, can you guess what the dragon said...?

THE END.

The MAGIC trick
By Leroy Lewis

I'm going to **SHARE** with you the *secret* of how I can make things disappear. This magic trick has been passed down from one magician to another over many **hundreds** of years.

Every magician learns this trick and is careful NEVER to give away the secret of how it's done.

So can YOU keep a secret?

GOOD! Because you are about to be **AMAZED.**

Say these magic words after me and wave your hands around at the same time...

Abracadabra – cadabra – BOO!

Now turn the page...

(It worked... See! Nothing there!)

I am a magician after all.

My Five-Star Funny Story
Great-Aunt Aggie's Fake Bird Hat
HA! HA!
by Tom Gates
HA! HA!

YES!

My story about *Great-Aunt Aggie's hat* got FIVE STARS from Mr Fullerman and made it into the book!

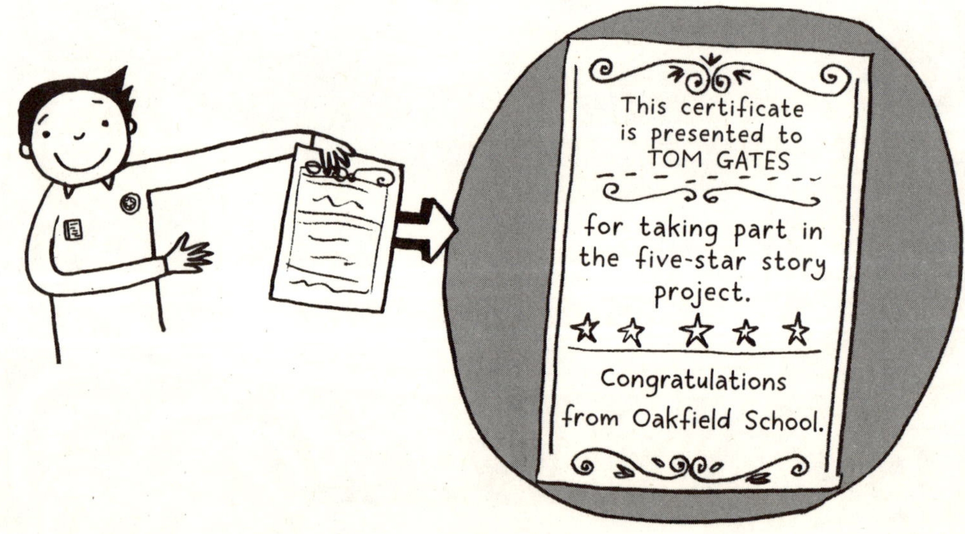

Mr Fullerman gave the WHOLE CLASS a certificate, a badge and a sticker for taking part in the FIVE-STAR STORY project even if your story didn't get in the book.

How brilliant is that?

(VERY.)

Derek's story about Rooster rolling in mud didn't get five stars, but he did get a SMILEY FACE on the class chart for being helpful.

That put him at the TOP of the chart, making him star pupil for the week.

His mum and dad gave him a little extra pocket money for doing so well. Derek told me he got a special pen (like mine) and a box of **Chocteezers**, which he's going to share.

(More good news!)

To celebrate the new book, we had a special assembly and some kids (not me) read out their stories and poems.

Buster Jones didn't want to read his story about **Mr Tedious** out. He pretended it wasn't his story.

(It was.)

Mr Keen said that <u>HE</u> would read the story instead, and when the

started LAUGHING at the silly names,

Buster looked surprised.

"Maybe I did write it after all," he admitted and enjoyed the round of applause at the end.

(I'm still not telling him I ate his **Chocteezers** though ... no need.)

When Mum and Dad saw the book, they **LOVED** it and didn't seem to mind I'd ordered **EXTRA** copies to give out to the family.

proud face

Delia said she didn't need one.

"No, thanks. What I'm hoping for is another decorated stone, Tom," she told me.

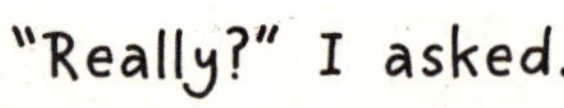

"Really?" I asked.

"No, I'm joking. And you'd better not have written a story about ME," she added.

"No, not this time. I wrote about Granddad's

Great-Aunt Aggie's hat."

Mum and Dad looked surprised like they didn't know.

"It's a FUNNY STORY, especially the bit about the CAT jumping on top of the hat and messing it all up so you had to FIX it, Mum!" I reminded them.

"Oh, yes. You've written it all down here, haven't you, Tom?" Mum said as she read the story.

"I have!"

"Maybe we shouldn't give a copy to Granddad yet. He still doesn't know exactly what happened to the hat," Mum told me

(a bit too late).

(Luckily THE FOSSILS were very impressed with Mum's "fixing" skills and they enjoyed my story.) ☺

Thanks to the book, there's a new CRAZE going around school where EVERYONE is trying to say Florence's song lyrics really fast without LAUGHING or making a mistake.

I'm not sure Mr Fullerman is enjoying the craze as much as we are.

Although I'm still playing the old game that Derek and I made up...

(Still looking...)

Draw a step-by-step BIRD from *Great-Aunt Aggie's* hat.

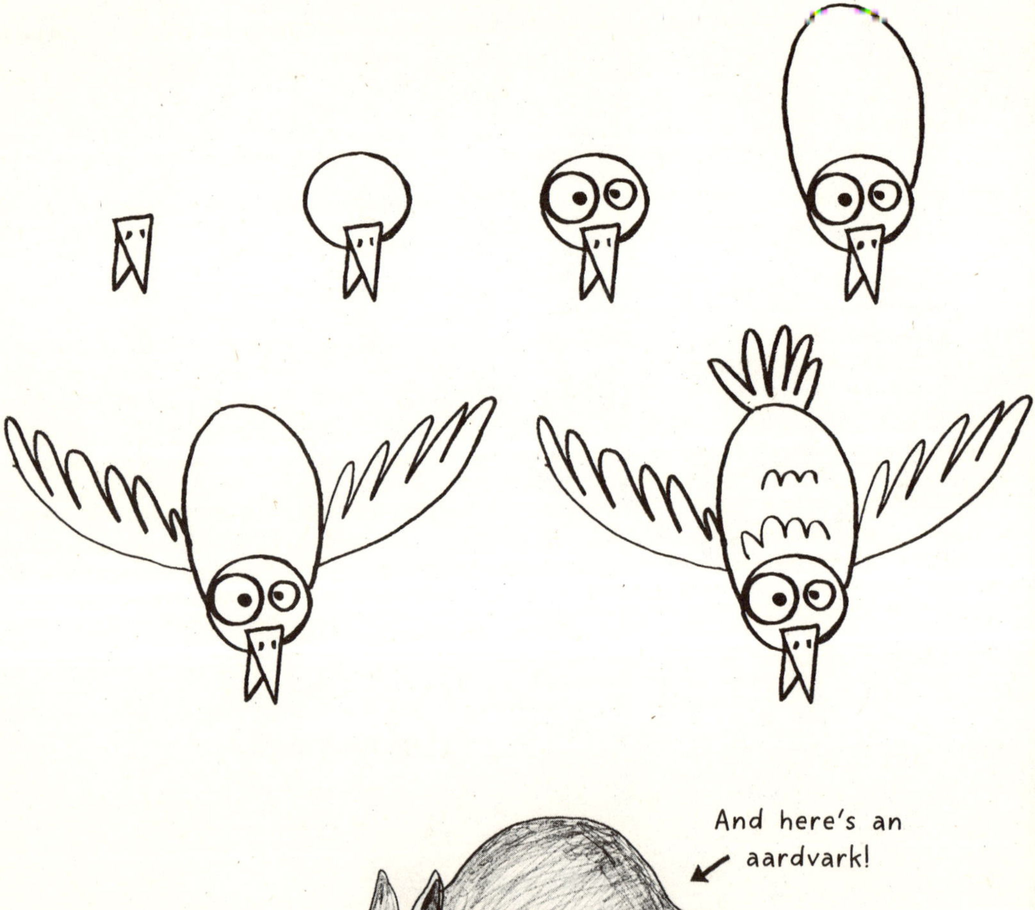

And here's an aardvark!

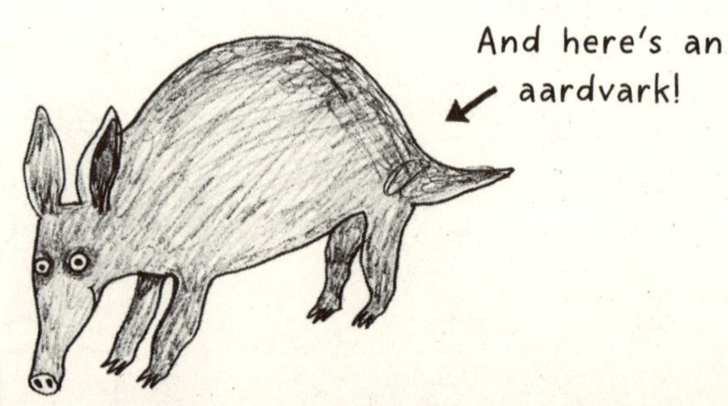

MAKE A CLAY BUG

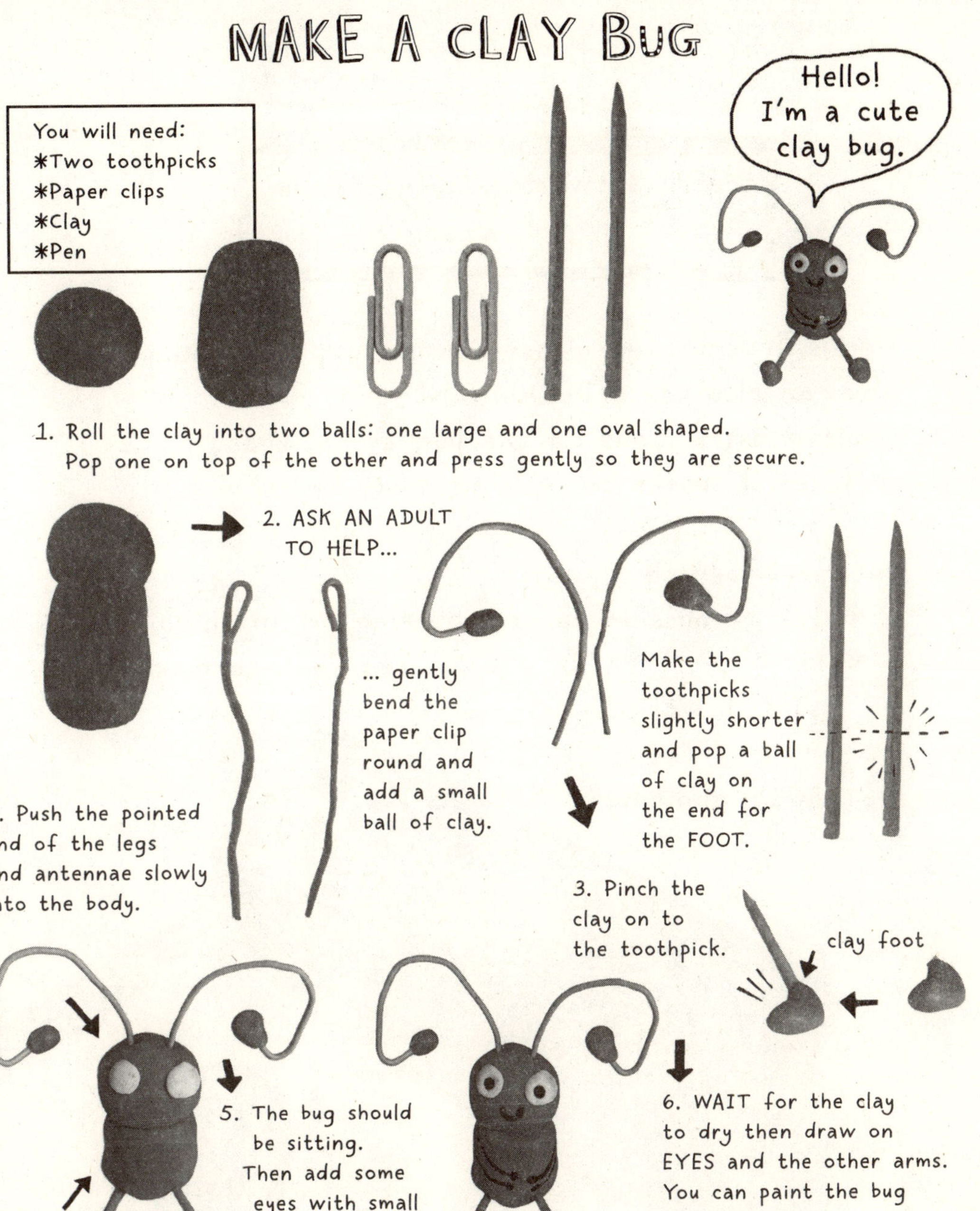

Here's a decorated glasses case using a special pen. You can also use a PERMANENT pen. (Follow instructions on the pen as to what surfaces it works on. Ask an adult to help.)

But remember to always:

* Get permission before drawing on anything.
* TEST your pen on a tiny area first to make sure it works.

GET BUSY doodling!

Star bug answers: the star bugs can be found on pages 40, 108, 127, 162 and 221.

LOOK! Here's the whole
Tom Gates collection.
How many have you read?
TOM GATES
The BRILLIANT WORLd OF TOM GATES
BY LIZ PICHON
TOM GATES
EXcellent ExcusEs
(and other good stuff)
BY LIZ PICHON
TOM GATES
Everything's AMAZING
BY LIZ PICHON
TOM GATES
GENIUS IDEAS
(mostly)
BY LIZ PICHON
TOM GATES
Absolutely FANTASTIC
BY LIZ PICHON
TOM GATES
EXTRA SPECIAL TREATS
(not)
BY LIZ PICHON
TOM GATES
A tiny Bit LUCKY
BY LIZ PICHON
TOM GATES
YES! NO. (Maybe...)
BY LIZ PICHON
TOM GATES
TOP of the CLASS
BY LIZ PICHON
TOM GATES
SUPER GOOD SKILLS
(almost)
BY LIZ PICHON
TOM GATES
DOG ZOMBIES RULE
(for now)
BY LIZ PICHON

www.thebrilliantworldoftomgates.com

YOU CAN DRAW

TOM GATES

WITH LIZ PICHON

From the BEST SELLING BOOKS and TV SERIES

Learn to draw step-by-step people, places and objects from Tom's world.

The must-have art activity book for fans of Tom Gates.

Read all the Tom Gates books?

Well now you can read ***SHOE WARS***, a standalone adventure story.

A Sunday Times Children's Book of the Year pick.

"Bursting with imagination and fabulous gadgets, ***Shoe Wars*** is full of Pichon's characteristic warmth, humour and quirky illustrations"
The Bookseller

"A tale oozing creativity and packed with pen and ink illustrations, exciting and expressive typography and visual jokes" *Booktrust*

Welcome to Shoe Town – and meet Ruby and Bear Foot. They are running out of time to rescue their inventor dad from his hideous boss, Wendy Wedge. She'll do ANYTHING to win the glitzy Golden Shoe Award and knows that entering flying shoes is her hot ticket to the trophy. Flying shoes that Ruby and Bear just happen to be hiding...

Liz Pichon is one of the UK's best-loved and bestselling creators of children's books.

Her TOM GATES series has been translated into 45 languages, sold millions of copies worldwide, and has won the Roald Dahl Funny Prize, the Blue Peter Book Award for Best Story and the younger fiction category of the Waterstones Children's Book Prize.

In the eleven years since THE BRILLIANT WORLD OF TOM GATES first published, the books have inspired the nation's children to get creative, whether that's through reading, drawing, doodling, writing, making music or performing.

"I wanted to FILL the books with ALL the things I loved doing when I was a kid. It's just the best feeling ever to know children are enjoying reading the books, because I love making them. So thank you so much for choosing Tom Gates and keep reading and doodling!"

(School photo of Liz being gru

Visit Liz at www.lizpichon.com